THE BEER LOVER'S TABLE

THE BEER LOVER'S TABLE

SEASONAL RECIPES AND MODERN BEER PAIRINGS

CLAIRE BULLEN WITH JEN FERGUSON

DOG 'n' BONE

Published in 2019 by Dog 'n' Bone Books
An imprint of Ryland Peters & Small Ltd
20–21 Jockey's Fields   341 E 116th St
London WC1R 4BW   New York, NY 10029
www.rylandpeters.com

10 9 8 7 6 5 4 3 2 1

A CIP catalog record for this book is available from the
Library of Congress and the British Library.

ISBN: 978 1 911026 78 5

Printed in China

Editor: Caroline West
Designer: Geoff Borin
Photographers: Matthew Curtis pages 2, 3, 9, 13, 18, 19, 23,
50, 51, 53, 84, 85, 87, 94, 98, 100, 112, 113, 115, 141, 144, 145,
147, 153, jacket spine photograph
Stephen Conroy pages 4 top, 5 bottom, 17, 33, 34, 45, 49, 58,
67, 70, 73, 78, 81, 90, 92, 97, 103, 106, 109, 110, 120, 123, 127,
131, 135, 137, 138, 142, 150, 154, 157, 158, 161, 164, 167, 168,
173, front cover photograph
Alex Luck pages 4 bottom, 5 top, 24, 29, 38, 41, 46, 57, 61,
74, 82
Additional photography: page 7 Daniel Batkin-Smith;
page 15 Shutterstock; pages 21 and 88 Allagash Brewing
Company; pages 31, 65, 68, 69 Loupe Images/Richard
Jung; page 37 Loupe Images/Peter Cassidy; page 55 Jack's
Abby Craft Lagers; pages 77 and p162 Loupe Images/Erin
Kunkel; page 105 Loupe Images/Martin Brigdale; page 116
Cloudwater Brew Co; p148 Claire Bullen
Stylist: Kim Sullivan
Home economists: Katy McClelland (Stephen Conroy
shots) and Laura Urschel (Alex Luck shots)

NOTE:
All spoon measurements are level, unless stated
otherwise. All eggs are US extra large (UK large)
and ideally free-range.

CONTENTS

FOREWORD
BY JEN FERGUSON

There's never been a better time to be a beer lover than right now. In almost every corner of the globe, beer is having a moment. From beer brewed 10,000 miles away to cans sourced from just up the road, beer lovers have never had more choice. What a time to be alive.

I've been lucky enough to enjoy great beer all over the world. Growing up in Nelson, New Zealand—home to some of the world's best hops—I was probably destined to love beer from an early age. However, it took 15 years of quantity-over-quality drinking in Kiwi booze barns and British pubs before I saw the light a decade ago, thanks to a bottle of Sierra Nevada Pale Ale. That beer helped me realize there was more to life than macro lager.

"Seeing the light" may sound somewhat dramatic, but ask any beer fan about the moment they fell for craft beer and you'll get a similar tale of epiphany. There's something about discovering craft beer that feels a little bit like gaining access to an exclusive (albeit wonderfully *inclusive*) club. Craft beer devotees may not remember exactly which beer tipped them over the edge, but they will recall the moment a whole new world of flavor and exploration opened up before them.

When my partner Glenn Williams and I got together in New Zealand in 2008, one of the many things we realized we had in common was a love of amazing beer. By the time we landed back in London five years later, we were spending most of our leisure time seeking out and drinking the best beer we could get our hands on, in all manner of weird and wonderful places. We'd plan travel itineraries around brewery tours, and the first place we'd seek out upon landing in a new town was the closest good beer bar.

It turns out chasing beer is an exceptionally good way to see the world and meet great people. We'd been welcomed in so many beer stores and bars that we wondered what it would be like to turn the tables and do the welcoming ourselves. So, inspired by the hoary old adage that "If you do what you love, it doesn't feel like work," in 2014 we quit our day jobs in order to open a specialist beer store called Hop Burns & Black, the original branch of which is located close to our home in Peckham Rye, south London.

We had three objectives in opening Hop Burns & Black: we wanted to create our own community hub where everyone felt welcome; we wanted to showcase and celebrate independent breweries and producers; and we wanted to surround ourselves with things we love and to share our passions with like-minded people. With that in mind, if we were going to sell beer, our first love, why not add our other obsessions to the mix? That's how we ended up with the world's first (and probably only) store for beer (the Hop), hot sauce (the Burns), and records (the Black). It may seem like something of a weird mix, but to us, these form a holy trinity—the meaning of life. Our fridge overflows with cans of beer and bottles of hot sauce, our shelves groan under the weight of vinyl—and we're not alone. Hop Burns & Black is now one of the UK's most successful and award-winning bottle stores, now with two south London outlets (Peckham and Deptford), plus an online store serving the obsessions of kindred spirits all over the country. (Cider and natural wine are also on our shelves—and our obsession list.)

Beer, however, has always taken center stage at Hop Burns & Black. When we opened in 2014, we were part of London's first wave of specialist craft beer stores—you could count them on one hand. The brewing scene, however, was thriving; there were 75 breweries based in London at the time and that figure has since increased to 120 and counting. This huge growth is reflected all over the world—as I type, it's been estimated there are close to 20,000 craft breweries globally. Putting aside the eternal argument over what constitutes a "craft brewery" for a moment, that's nothing less than a sea change.

Faced with this explosion of choice, people began to look at beer differently, and stores like ours offered the perfect opportunity to go exploring. Our customers may not have started out as beer connoisseurs, but they quickly became so. Enthusiasm for craft beer is contagious. Like us, our customers wanted to discover new breweries, explore different styles, push boundaries, and show off their good taste to friends. They also wanted to involve beer in more areas of their lives—and nowhere more so than at the dinner table.

Enter Claire Bullen, beer lover and food writer extraordinaire. Introduced to us by our mutual friend, beer writer and photographer Matthew Curtis (whose photographs you'll find in this book), Claire started working with Hop Burns & Black in 2015, when we commissioned her to write a regular column—The Beer Lover's Table—on food and beer pairings.

With The Beer Lover's Table, we didn't want to replicate the "dude food" recipes that litter the Internet when you search for "beer and food pairings." While we love Buffalo wings as much as the next person, we wanted to enjoy beer alongside a wider range of meals, from vibrant spaghetti for #PastaMonday nights on the sofa to simple salads during summer nights in the backyard, or grilled pork belly dinners with friends. We wanted great food to accompany great beers, and we wanted to explore the huge potential that beer, in all its styles and infinite complexity, offers as a culinary partner.

In Claire, we knew we'd found a superstar. Her writing is warm, witty, and inclusive; her recipes sophisticated and yet simple enough for most to make. Her dishes are inspirational and aspirational, but not intimidating or pretentious, and they're all expertly matched with complementary beers. Claire's column soon became the most popular content on our blog, so I was delighted when we had the opportunity to put it into print. In addition to Claire's wonderful recipes, I'm happy for the chance to wax lyrical about my all-consuming passion for beer throughout.

SO WHAT THE HECK IS CRAFT BEER ANYWAY?

Ah, the age-old question. For years, the beer industry has been tying itself in knots trying to find a single, commonly held definition of "craft beer." The Brewers Association in the US defines a craft brewery as small (with an annual production of 6 million barrels of beer or fewer); independent (less than 25 percent owned or controlled by a member of the alcohol industry that is not a craft brewer); and traditional (the majority of beers must derive their flavors from traditional or innovative brewing ingredients and fermentation).

However, we find "craft" to be a bit more nebulous. For us, the term refers to an ethos: it's about beer that's well-crafted, made with care and passion, and brewed

by good people (we have no qualms about hauling beer off shelves if we see sexist labeling or learn that staff are being mistreated). It's also hugely important to us as an independent retailer to support other independent businesses. It's at the very core of our mission.

Over the past few years, multinational beverage conglomerates ("Big Beer") have made huge inroads into the independent craft scene, snapping up high-profile breweries from around the world and posing a serious threat to the industry. With every influential craft brewery that the likes of AB InBev or Heineken take a stake in, the more the market is tied up, and the harder it is for us and our indie friends to make a living. For that reason, we choose not to sell beers made by breweries owned by Big Beer, and, barring one or two notable exceptions, have chosen independent breweries to feature in this book. Having said that, the landscape is changing quickly, with craft breweries being bought up regularly, so we can't guarantee this will be the case by the time this book is published!

Essentially, craft beer wouldn't exist without the tireless work of independent breweries, bars, and stores all around the world. We hope you'll do your part to support the ongoing health and diversity of this wonderfully vibrant industry by buying indie whenever you can. That indie-brewed beers taste all the sweeter with food is one more bonus.

INTRODUCTION
BY CLAIRE BULLEN

A specific kind of magic happens when good food and good beer get together. I noticed it for the first time seven years ago, while visiting a Belgian beer bar in Brooklyn. At the time, I was a trainee beer walking-tour guide, shadowing my boss on a trip around the borough. A group of us squeezed around the bar's largest table, each with a plate of cheese and a flight of beers before us. We were hungry, after an afternoon spent walking and drinking, but we listened as my boss told us to wait and try each pairing individually.

One pairing stood out in particular: an aged Gouda cheese the color of butterscotch alongside a potent barley wine. Individually, both were exceptional, but together, they were transformed. The sweetness of the barley wine drew out the abundant nutty, toffee notes in the cheese. The Gouda, meanwhile, added balance to the beer and focused its more delicate, hoppy aromas. The two even complemented each other texturally: both were rich and mouth-coating, but the aged Gouda's protein crystals added an irresistible crunch between the teeth, a burst of salt that demanded a chaser. I loved beer, and I loved food… but I didn't realize they could do this.

For most of us, beer and food are found together in moments of casual recreation. Pairings rarely exist in a way that is carefully considered, or elevated beyond pub grub. Beer is generally not what you order at fine restaurants, nor is it what you bring to dinner parties. Beer's province has traditionally been the game, barbecues, happy hour. To discover that beer could do more than just refresh and intoxicate—that it could elevate and transform food—was a small but powerful revelation to me.

As we continued to taste, my boss thumbed through the bar's bookshelf, in search of a particular volume. He pulled out *The Brewmaster's Table*. Written by Brooklyn Brewery's brewmaster Garrett Oliver in 2005, it was one of the first books to deal with the subject of food and beer pairings in a methodical, knowledgeable, deeply impassioned way. My boss read from the introduction:

"Mexican, Thai, Japanese, Indian, Cajun, and Middle Eastern food, and barbecue, are far better with real beer than with wine. Even with traditionally wine-friendly foods, beer often shows superior versatility and flavor compatibility. The range of flavors and aromas in beer is vast—it's deep and wide and tall, and it easily surpasses that of wine. Beer has bitterness to slice through fat, carbonation to refresh the palate, caramelized flavors to match those in our food, and sweetness to quench the fire of chilies."

From that moment onward—and later, when I became a fully fledged walking-tour guide, and served beer and cheese to my own groups—I kept coming back to the idea of beer's culinary potential. I'd always been a curious and dedicated home cook. I bought my own copy of *The Brewmaster's Table* and, in my shared apartment kitchen, started to pair beer with the dishes I made, in search of harmonious matches. Not all the combinations worked—chocolate stouts and Thai curries are not destined to be together—but many of them did. I started to invite friends over for dinner, and served meals exclusively with beer on the side: no wine allowed.

I don't mean to fan the flames of the beer-versus-wine debate, by the way—I love wine. But I'd always considered the world of wine pairings to be esoteric and forbidding to newcomers. Beer instead offers a fantastic freedom. There are no elaborate metrics to memorize when it comes to creating pairings, and few sacrosanct rules. The topic is new enough that there's ample room for experimentation. That world-class beer is increasingly available in bars, breweries, and bottle stores all over, much of it sold for mere pocket change, makes it especially accessible.

DEFENDING FOOD AND BEER PAIRINGS

It's a shame, then, that more than a decade after *The Brewmaster's Table* was published, Oliver's wisdom still needs defending. Many of the wine drinkers I know persist in thinking of beer as simplistic and without nuance, more appropriate for late-night parties than dinnertime pairings. On the other hand, I'm also acquainted with beer drinkers who dismiss beer and food pairings as overly fussy and contrived. They worry that bringing beer to the dinner table contributes to its

"wineification" and lends it an elitist, pretentious air.

Respectfully, I think both camps have it wrong. Beer's tremendous versatility and range make it possible to find a fitting pairing for virtually any dish, whether sweet or savory, comforting or challenging, spicy or subtle. Sea bass ceviche pairs dreamily with hefeweizen, while basil-perfumed gueuze is in a league of its own alongside caprese salad. And what wine could surpass a tropical double IPA as a pairing for shrimp and mango curry?

Beer pairings shouldn't feel precious or forced—they couldn't be more natural. How lucky for us that we live in a golden age of beery abundance, and have an ever-broadening palette to pick from. These days, bourbon barrel-aged stouts share fridge space with hazy New England IPAs, bottle shops sell mixed-fermentation sours alongside crystal-clear pilsners, and goses and saisons pour side by side.

THE BEGINNINGS OF THE BEER LOVER'S TABLE

Skip forward to 2014 when I was newly arrived in London, and ready for a change of scenery and a different city to call home. I was dismayed at first to discover that, compared to New York, London had very few dedicated craft beer bars and bottle stores. But then Hop Burns & Black opened. At the time, its wide-ranging bottle selection, and warm welcome, felt thrilling to discover. I soon found myself making regular pilgrimages to south London to pick up supplies, attend events, and catch up with its hospitable owners, Jen and Glenn. And while it's no longer alone in the wilderness—London's beer scene has blossomed enormously in the space of a few years—Hop Burns & Black still sets the standard for all that a bottle shop can be.

When Jen approached me three years ago with the opportunity to write a column for Hop Burns & Black, beer and food pairings was the first topic that sprang to mind. Named with a nod to Garrett Oliver's book, The Beer Lover's Table column has since become a freewheeling opportunity to explore beer's culinary potential, to pair some of my favorite beers with an array of eclectic dishes, and to give those who are new to beer an accessible medium with which to discover it.

OUR AIMS FOR THIS BOOK

With that spirit of exploration in mind, we have a few objectives for this book. Firstly, we're banishing the stodgy clichés and are instead featuring dishes that might not be considered typical "beer food." The following recipes represent the curious and varied way that we—and our food-loving, city-dwelling friends and peers—eat today. In lieu of shepherd's pie and jalapeño poppers, you'll find dishes like Vietnamese Pork Belly (see page 60), Nectarine Panzanella Salad (see page 118), and Shawarma-spiced Cauliflower (see page 107). Many recipes also reflect a seasonal perspective, so you have an excuse to visit the local greengrocer or farmers' market and find a use for the new-season tomatoes, asparagus, or cherries that have just arrived.

We're also breaking from the standard that has guided other beer-centric cookbooks and are leaving beer out of the recipes. As an ingredient, beer can be tricky to work with, but as a pairing partner, it reliably adds a compelling new dimension to a meal.

The recipes in the book aren't meant to be strictly prescriptive: there are infinite creative ways to pair beer with food. Think of them instead as illustrations of all that beer can do in a dining context, and also as encouragement to craft pairings of your own.

To guide your explorations further, at the start of each chapter we've drawn up a chart of beer styles and the dishes and flavors they pair well with to use as a general reference tool. We've also compiled a Glossary (see pages 11–13) of essential beer terminology, plus a guide to the most common varieties of hops you're likely to come across (see Key Hop Varieties, pages 15–16). Don't miss the seasonal dinner party menus, which are designed to inspire your at-home hospitality, plus the detailed beer style guides at the start of each chapter.

All this information is intended to open up the world of beer and food pairings, rather than limit you to certain narrow formulas. Inviting beer to the dinner table should be accessible rather than self-conscious, experimental rather than strict, fun rather than fussy. Sample widely, craft unexpected combinations, and see what happens. If you're passionate about good food and obsessed with beer, then it only makes sense to bring the two of them together at the table.

GLOSSARY

ABV: Alcohol by volume, or the alcoholic content of a beverage. ABV in beer can range from below 1% in low-alcohol styles up to 14% (or higher) in eisbocks and barrel-aged stouts.

Adjunct: Any source of fermentable sugars in a beer that isn't malted grain. This can include unmalted grains like barley, wheat, corn, and rice, as well as Belgian candi sugar, honey, maple syrup, pumpkins, stone fruit, and beyond.

Ale: A beer brewed with top-fermenting ale yeast (*Saccharomyces cerevisiae*), which ferments relatively quickly and at warm temperatures. Ale is a broad category that encompasses numerous beer styles.

Alpha acids: The acids contained in a hop's lupulin glands that make hops—and consequently beer—bitter. The higher the percentage of alpha acids, the more intense the bitterness.

Barrel-aging: The storage of beer in wooden barrels for months (and up to many years) at a time. Barrels formerly used to store wine and spirits are popular among brewers, as they impart new flavors and complexity to beer. Barrels also provide an environment for mixed-fermentation beers to develop and mature.

Body: A beer's consistency and viscosity. Pilsners, for example, have a light, thin body, whereas barley wines are rich and full-bodied.

Brettanomyces: Often shortened to Brett, a wild yeast that is frequently found in mixed-fermentation beers. Its funky, earthy, and highly distinctive flavor and aroma is often described as "barnyard-y."

Carbonation: One of beer's key characteristics, ranging from subtle to explosive. Carbon dioxide (CO_2) is produced naturally during primary and secondary fermentations; some beer is also force-carbonated (directly infused with CO_2) prior to packaging.

Coolship: A flat, shallow vessel that is left open to the air to allow wort to cool and be inoculated by airborne yeasts and bacteria. Coolships (also spelled koelschips) are common among Belgian lambic producers.

Dry hopping: The process of adding additional hops to a beer while it is fermenting or conditioning. The primary goal of dry hopping is to impart beer with vibrant hop flavors and aromatics. When two rounds of dry-hopping additions are used, this is known as double dry hopping (often abbreviated as "DDH").

Esters: Flavor compounds produced as a by-product of fermentation. Esters often taste fruity or floral; banana esters, for instance, are a notable component of hefeweizens.

Fermentation: A natural process that occurs when yeast consumes sugars and produces alcohol, carbon dioxide, and other flavor compounds. Simply put, fermentation is what transforms sugar water into beer.

Fermentation vessel: Also known as FVs, fermentation vessels are used to contain the inoculated wort as it undergoes fermentation and transforms into beer.

Fining and filtration: Fining involves introducing an agent to beer which binds with yeast and proteins and removes them from suspension. This process produces a clarified beer. Filtration is the process of filtering a beer through a porous material to remove particles and produce a clarified final product. Many craft beers are neither filtered nor fined.

Finish: The flavor and sensation left on the palate after a beer has been swallowed. A beer's finish can be subtle or pronounced, short or long, dry or sweet, and more.

Foudre: Originally borrowed from the wine world, foudres are extra-large wooden barrels that brewers primarily use to age mixed-fermentation beers.

Gravity: The measure of fermentable and non-fermentable sugars present in a beer. The original gravity (OG) is taken prior to fermentation, while the final gravity (FG) is measured afterward. Subtracting the FG from the OG helps determine a beer's ABV.

Haze: Haze, or turbidity, exists in beer that is unfiltered, and is common to many traditional styles. Today, hazy IPAs (also referred to as East Coast IPAs, New England IPAs, or NEIPAs) are enormously popular. In these polarizing beers—typically made with oats and wheat—haze is often the result of hop polyphenols binding with proteins and remaining in suspension (colloidal haze). Many brewers and drinkers argue that filtering this beer would change its flavor, and, in some circles, haze has become the marker of a delicious, boldly flavored IPA.

Head: The foam top on a beer, linked to carbonation. Some styles, like hefeweizens and witbiers, are known for their robust and fluffy heads; many cask ales, on the other hand, have less head retention.

Hops/hoppy: Hops are one of beer's four major ingredients, alongside water, yeast, and malt. The cone flowers of large climbing plants, hops contain bitterness, possess antimicrobial properties, and, most importantly, have a huge range of flavors and aromas. Hops are grown all over the world and each strain has its own unique character. Many styles of beer rely heavily on hops for their flavor, including pale ales, IPAs, and double IPAs. "Hoppy" is a somewhat vague beer descriptor, however, and is used to refer to both hop aromatics and bitterness.

IBU: International Bittering Units, used to measure the alpha acids (and therefore the bitterness) present in a beer.

Kettle: A key piece of brewing equipment—the vessel in which wort is boiled alongside several hop additions.

Kettle souring: As opposed to sour mixed-fermentation beers, which ferment over the course of months or years, kettle sours can be made in a matter of days. After the wort is transferred to the kettle and cooled to a certain temperature, it is inoculated with *Lactobacillus* bacteria, which produces lactic acid.

Lactobacillus: This bacteria imparts sourness to beer and is the same kind of bacteria that is found in yogurt and cheese. *Lactobacillus* is used to make kettle sours and is also frequently found in mixed-fermentation cultures.

Lager: Beer brewed with bottom-fermenting lager yeast (*Saccharomyces pastorianus*) and fermented slowly at cold temperatures.

Lagering: The cold storing of beer after fermentation and before filtration or packaging.

Malt/malty: Malt is another core component of beer, along with hops, yeast, and water. To produce malt, grains—most commonly barley, but also frequently wheat or rye—are germinated, kilned, and then roasted to varying degrees. Malt provides color and a range of sweet and roasted flavors, as well as sugars, which the yeast consumes during fermentation. When a beer is described as "malty," it usually means its sweetness and malty flavors (including biscuit, caramel, and toasty notes) are at the fore.

Mashing in: At the start of the brewing process, hot water (liquor) is added to the malt (typically barley, wheat, and/or rye) in the mash tun—a process which converts the starches into fermentable sugars. This porridge-like mix of grains and hot water is known as the mash, and this process is called mashing in.

Mash tun and lauter tun: The vessels used in the first stages of the brewing process. Hot water (liquor) is added to the malt in the mash tun to create the mash. Next, the mash is transferred to the lauter tun, where solids are filtered from the wort.

Mixed fermentation: The term for beer that is fermented using multiple strains of yeast and bacteria, including *Saccharomyces cerevisiae*, *Brettanomyces*, *Lactobacillus*, *Pediococcus*, and other microbes. Mixed-fermentation beers typically take months or years to produce, and are known for their complex, often sour, flavors.

Mouthfeel: The physical feel of a beer in the mouth. Mouthfeel can be creamy, chewy, effervescent, soft, and more.

Pasteurization: The process of heating beer to a high temperature in order to destroy bacteria and prolong its shelf life.

Pediococcus: Often shortened to Pedio. A bacteria used in sour beer brewing, frequently alongside *Brettanomyces*. It contributes lactic acid as well as funky flavors and aromas, and is a key ingredient in lambics and Flanders red ales.

Phenols: Flavor and aroma compounds produced during fermentation, often described as spicy, clovey, smoky, medicinal, or even Band-Aid-(plaster)-like. Desirable in some beers, such as hefeweizen; perceived as an off-flavor in other styles.

Reinheitsgebot: The "Purity Law" that controls which ingredients can be used in German beer (see right). It was introduced by the Duke of Bavaria more than 500 years ago and still exists today, though not all breweries abide by it. Originally it permitted barley, hops, and water only; nowadays, it incorporates yeast, additional malted grains, and several other ingredients.

Residual sugars: Sugars that are still present in beer after fermentation is complete. A beer with a lot of residual sugar will be fuller and sweeter; one with less residual sugar will be drier and lighter.

Saccharomyces cerevisiae: A yeast used in the production of ale styles. It ferments more quickly and at higher temperatures than lager yeast. Because it rises to the surface of the beer during fermentation, it's known as a top-fermenting yeast.

Saccharomyces pastorianus: A yeast used in the production of lager. It works best in cooler temperatures and ferments much more slowly than ale yeast, producing fewer fermentation by-products such as esters, and a "cleaner" beer. Because lager yeast tends to sink to the bottom of the beer, it is described as bottom-fermenting.

Secondary fermentation: Refers to any form of fermentation that takes place once the primary fermentation—during which newly boiled wort is freshly inoculated with yeast cultures—has occurred. Secondary fermentation can take place in bottles (when additional yeast cultures and sugars are added), conditioning tanks, casks, or other vessels. The process can create additional carbonation and mellow out unwanted off-flavors in some styles.

Spontaneous fermentation: Fermentation that occurs when beer is inoculated with wild yeasts and bacteria, rather than a pitched culture. Coolships aid in the process of spontaneous fermentation by exposing wort to cultures in the air.

Water/liquor: Along with hops, malt, and yeast, this is one of the core elements of beer. Water can drastically affect the taste of beer due to differences in pH levels and mineral content, so brewers use a range of techniques, such as filtration and mineral additions, to achieve the water quality and consistency they require.

Wort: The sweet liquid derived from the mashing-in process. After filtering or lautering, the wort is transferred to the kettle to be boiled, during which hops are added prior to fermentation.

Yeast: Yeast is a microorganism that converts sugars to produce alcohol, CO_2, and other flavor compounds such as esters and phenols. It contributes significantly to the flavor of some beer styles, such as wheat beers, and adds haze to the likes of wheat beers and New England IPAs when not filtered out.

ESSENTIAL PRINCIPLES OF FOOD AND BEER PAIRING

Why does beer pair so well with food? Quite simply, its enormous variety of flavors, aromas, and ingredients make it phenomenally versatile. Malted grains lend it a caramelized sweetness, roasty flavors, and nuttiness. Hops impart bitterness, boldness, and vibrant aromatics. Yeast, especially German and Belgian varieties, bestows fruit and spice notes. Bacteria add sourness, while barrel-aging gives beer richness, a luxurious mouthfeel, and woodiness. Additional ingredients, ranging from fruits and spices to coffee—and even shellfish—contribute yet another vector of flavor.

In short, as Garrett Oliver notes in *The Brewmaster's Table*, "You can easily see that beer is an amazingly complex beverage, so it is not surprising that beer has so much to offer food." But don't feel intimidated by beer's multitudes. Instead, follow these basic pairing principles, which make it easy to craft a successful match.

Intensity
Arguably the most important factor to consider when matching food and beer is intensity: in most cases, you're after a pairing in which each element engages the other, an equal dialogue between parties. Pair delicate white fish with a barrel-aged stout, and the fish's subtle flavors and aromatics will be completely overwhelmed by the beer's strength and richness. Likewise, robust, braised short ribs would obliterate the gentle froth and whisper of coriander in a witbier. Instead, try the witbier and the white fish together, and pair the short ribs and the stout—both are well matched in terms of impact, boldness, and intensity.

Complementary pairings
Once you've matched your pairings by intensity, there's room to experiment further. One foolproof method is to pair like with like, and marry complementary flavors. A sweet chocolate stout and a slice of chocolate cake, for instance, are a tried-and-true duo. A tart, briny gose is a natural alongside fresh seafood dishes. To forge a complementary match, seek out beers and dishes that share flavors (or even ingredients).

Contrasting pairings
Contrasting food and beer pairings can also work splendidly. Keep richness, acidity, and bitterness in mind: to contrast the creaminess of a chocolate mousse, for example, turn to a raspberry lambic, whose tartness and bright fruit notes provide a counterbalancing effect. Spicy dishes, meanwhile, don't tend to pair well with IPAs, as the style's hoppy bitterness only enhances the heat. Instead, a sweeter, maltier style, like a brown ale, helps put out the flames. That hoppy IPA is better used as a foil for rich, unctuous dishes; its bitterness cuts through fat like a hot knife through butter.

Carbonation and mouthfeel
Often overlooked in favor of flavor and aromatics, mouthfeel—beer's viscosity and carbonation, literally the way it feels on the palate—can have a significant impact on pairings. Highly carbonated beers, such as lagers, weissbiers, and bottle-conditioned Belgian styles, are excellent with creamy and mouth-coating dishes, as the bubbles help to "scrub" the palate clean between bites. On the complementary side, a beer with a viscous and rich mouthfeel pairs well with a similarly indulgent cheese or dessert.

Proximity and seasonality
"What grows together, goes together" is an old adage used for food and wine pairings. While this concept doesn't directly translate to beer—terroir in beer is usually less distinct than in wine, as the component ingredients can hail from all over the world—there are still cases in which traditional, location-specific styles pair well with food from the same respective regions. Consider the harmony between German rauchbiers and local smoked meats, or French saisons and boudin blanc. Likewise, beers made with seasonal ingredients—pumpkin beers, fruit-infused sours—tend to pair well with comparably seasonal dishes.

KEY HOP VARIETIES

Hops go a long way toward creating a beer's flavor and aroma; as such, they're important to consider when crafting food and beer pairings. Each hop variety has its own signature characteristics and, broadly speaking, can taste and smell like anything from zesty citrus to resinous pine and tropical fruit. Some hops even have notes of onion and garlic. While new strains are released all the time, this list includes those hop varieties you're most likely to encounter.

Amarillo: An American aroma hop that first debuted in 2000, Amarillo is prized for its citrusy, apricot-like fragrance and even more intense flavor. On the palate, it's boldly fruity, and tastes distinctively of orange.

Azacca: Named for the Haitian god of agriculture, Azacca is an unabashedly fruit-forward hop variety, and is used as both a bittering and aroma hop. Its predominant tropical-fruit notes are balanced with a dose of citrus and pine.

Bramling Cross: A traditional, dual-purpose English hop variety, Bramling Cross isn't the newest kid on the block, but its distinctive blackcurrant and lemon profile lends it a subtle and refined character.

Cascade: Released in the early 1970s, Cascade is one of the five so-called "C hops" that have, in the ensuing decades, played a foundational role in the American craft beer revolution. Its flavor profile pairs pithy grapefruit with resinous pine, and, as a dual-purpose hop, it's a common choice for American pale ales.

Centennial: Another original C hop, Centennial is often described as "super Cascade." It is citrusy and piney, with an added floral quality; a more intense bitterness makes it well-suited to West Coast IPAs and double IPAs.

Chinook: Primarily used as a bittering hop, C hop #3, Chinook, has a spicy grapefruit character. More recently, brewers have begun to dry hop with Chinook, a process which emphasizes its herbaceous, piney characteristics.

Citra: A phenomenally popular dual-purpose hop, Citra was developed in the 1990s and is extraordinarily, vividly potent. On the nose, it's ripe with exotic fruit and citrus.

Citra can also take on a pungent, slightly savory profile, especially during dry hopping.

Columbus: The last of the C hops, Columbus is also sometimes labeled as Tomahawk, and is very similar to another hop called Zeus; as such, it's often known as "CTZ." A potent bittering hop, Columbus also provides pungent, resinous—even dank—aromatics.

Denali: One of the newest hop strains on this list, Denali was only released in 2016. Named after North America's tallest mountain, it's big and bold in every way. Expect super-juicy pineapple and tropical-fruit characteristics, alongside pine and citrus.

East Kent Golding: Among the most classic and revered English hop breeds, East Kent Golding has centuries of history behind it. This dual-purpose hop has an earthy, grassy profile, and is a classic choice for traditional English ales.

Ekuanot: Originally called Equinox, this hop underwent a name change following a legal dispute. Ekuanot is known for its bright, lemon-lime flavor, with added papaya and apple aromatics. Occasionally, tasters have also detected green bell (sweet) pepper notes.

El Dorado: El Dorado offers a bouquet of fruity flavors: tropical mango and pineapple mingle with apricot and cherry. This dual-purpose hop also has a distinct, watermelon accent that can make it taste almost candied in some contexts.

Ella: The hop formerly known as Stella (before falling foul to legal pressure), Ella is Australian-bred and mingles floral notes with a subtly spicy, star-anise character. When dry hopped, its grapefruit notes come to the fore.

Enigma: Another up-and-coming Australian varietal, the aptly named Enigma has a complex, chameleonic range of characteristics. Some taste raspberry and blackcurrant notes, while others detect tropical fruit or white wine.

Fuggle: Another centuries-old English hop variety, Fuggle is primarily used as an aroma hop in contemporary brewing, and has a restrained, earthy, woody character.

Galaxy: The star of the Australian hop industry, Galaxy is beloved by brewers for its ripe array of peach, mango, pineapple, basil, and citrus flavors and aromas.

Hallertau Blanc: Not to be confused with the noble hop below, Hallertau Blanc is a modern German hop that's descended from Cascade. First released in 2012, it's recognizable for its grape, gooseberry, elderflower, and cassis notes, and is often likened to a white wine.

Hallertauer Mittelfrüh: Hallertauer Mittelfrüh, which hails from Germany, is one of four so-called "noble hops": classic, continental European varieties. With its floral aroma and spicy character, it's a subtle and refined hop.

Huell Melon: Another contemporary German creation, Huell Melon, as its name suggests, boasts a bright honeydew character. Strawberry, vanilla, and apricot notes might also be detected.

Loral: Described as a "super-noble hop," Loral—released in 2016—is floral and herbaceous. It also has added complexity courtesy of dark-fruit and tea notes.

Mandarina Bavaria: As its name implies, Mandarina Bavaria is both of German origin and tastes of mandarin oranges, tangerines, and other bright citrus fruits.

Mosaic: Alongside Citra, Mosaic is another wildly popular hop that has become a near-ubiquitous addition to contemporary IPAs. Like Citra and Simcoe, it ably mingles bright mango and stone-fruit notes with a musky, savory, allium backbone.

Motueka: Tutti-frutti Motueka, which hails from Nelson, New Zealand, features a pleasing lemon-lime character alongside lively tropical-fruit aromatics.

Nelson Sauvin: One of New Zealand's most in-demand hop varieties, Nelson Sauvin is often described as having a vinous character. As with the Sauvignon Blanc grape, which is produced in the same region, it's known for its gooseberry, lychee, and passion-fruit notes.

Saaz: Another noble hop, Saaz—which hails from the Czech Republic—is a classic addition to the pilsners of the region. This aroma hop has an herbal earthiness and subtly spicy character.

Simcoe: A popular hop variety in IPAs, super-aromatic Simcoe is perfect for those who like a savory quality in their beers. Its musky, citrusy profile can at times veer toward the dank and pungent; some drinkers even detect onion or garlic notes.

Sorachi Ace: Polarizing Sorachi Ace has a very distinctive flavor profile; many tasters detect whiffs of lemon, a buttery oakiness, dill, coconut, and orange. Primarily used as a bittering hop, its unique aromatic qualities please some and repel others.

Spalt: Spalt, another noble hop, hails from Germany. Like its counterparts, Spalt is known for its refined and nuanced profile, which leans toward the earthy and subtly spicy. It's a popular choice in altbiers.

Tettnanger: The fourth and final noble hop, Tettnanger comes from southern Germany, and is a prized aroma hop. Expect grapefruit, grassy, and herbal characteristics.

Vic Secret: Named because it originally hailed from Victoria, Australia, Vic Secret is like a mild-mannered Galaxy. Expect tropical-fruit, passion-fruit, and herbal notes.

Wai-iti: Prized for its intensely aromatic profile, Wai-iti is all lime and lemon on the nose; when brewed, it often adds ripe peach and apricot aromatics.

Wakatu: A descendant of Hallertauer Mittelfrüh, the New Zealand-bred Wakatu features an appealing floral, vanilla profile with notes of fresh citrus. It also has good bittering potential.

SEASONAL DINNER PARTY MENUS

SPRING

Starter Sea Bass Ceviche (page 96)
PAIR WITH An orange- or grapefruit-infused wheat beer

Main Spring Orecchiette (page 32)
PAIR WITH A light, citrusy kettle-soured beer

Dessert Vanilla Panna Cotta with Rhubarb Compote (page 44)
PAIR WITH A sweet, berry-infused lambic

SUMMER

Starter Tomato and Strawberry Salad (page 91)
PAIR WITH A spice-led wheat beer

Main Vietnamese Pork Belly with Noodles, Frizzled Shallots, and Watermelon Salad (page 60)
PAIR WITH A Bavarian pilsner

Dessert Peach Upside-down Cake with Miso Caramel (page 140)
PAIR WITH A West Coast-style IPA

FALL (AUTUMN)

Starter Cheddar and Chive Biscuits with Tomato Jam (page 30)
PAIR WITH A bready, biscuity saison

Main Roast Quail and Squash with Yogurt Sauce and Hazelnut Gremolata (page 160)
PAIR WITH A Belgian dubbel

Dessert Pistachio Saffron Cupcakes (page 143)
PAIR WITH A malt-driven pale ale or IPA

WINTER

Starter Shawarma-spiced Cauliflower with Pomegranate and Tahini Sauce (page 107)
PAIR WITH A dunkelweizen

Main Beer-braised Short Ribs (page 162)
PAIR WITH A Belgian dubbel

Dessert Blondies with Sweet Potato Ripple (page 108)
PAIR WITH A sweet, dark wheat beer

CHAPTER 1 | SOURS AND SAISONS

GUIDE TO SOURS AND SAISONS BY JEN FERGUSON

Each and every time you drink a beer, you're enjoying the results of a process that dates back hundreds of years. Modern breweries may be all shiny stainless steel and technological wizardry, but the fundamentals of beer remain the same—it's still produced using a combination of hops, malt, water, and yeast, transformed inexorably by fermentation. That's why I think it's fitting this book begins with two types of beer that owe so much to historical brewing methods. Sours and saisons are rich in tradition, yet serve as natural companions to modern meals.

"Sours" is something of an umbrella term that groups together a range of very different styles of beer, all made in very different ways. As a flavor descriptor, it's a bit vague, too: from the briny brightness of a gose to the funky complexity of a gueuze or the almost vinegar-like tartness of a Flanders red, there's a wide spectrum of sourness out there. And, while we've separated them out here, it's worth noting that saisons can sometimes be sour, too.

Personally, I love them all. Some of my happiest beer memories involve savoring a spritzy gose in the sunshine with friends or getting the "sour sweats" with a big tart lambic. They're wonderful on their own or—even better—as part of a well-paired meal that brings both the beer and the food alive.

SOUR BELGIAN STYLES

Back in the day—before the mid-19th century—nearly all beer would have been sour, due to a lack of both refrigeration and knowledge of microorganisms and the science of fermentation. While sourness was sometimes considered an off-flavor (an unfortunate side effect of rudimentary brewing), some brewers made an art form out of wild and funky fermentation.

At Cantillon Brewery in Brussels, you can see this age-old brewing process firsthand, little changed from yesteryear. Large, shallow coolships (flat, open-top vessels) are filled with newly brewed wort and left open

to the air to be inoculated by wild yeasts and bacteria. Then, the liquid is transferred to wooden barrels or large oak foudres, where it ferments and matures over the course of months, if not years. The result is earthy, strongly sour lambic beer. Some lambics are fermented with fruits, while other lambics of varying ages are blended to make refined, wonderfully complex gueuze, which is often considered beer's equivalent to Champagne.

Today, lambics are some of the world's most in-demand beers. Bottles from breweries such as Cantillon, 3 Fonteinen, and Tilquin, regularly change hands for enormous sums on the trading market (much to the chagrin of the brewers in question). They're not for the faint-hearted but, like any acquired taste, these beers offer drinkers a wonderful new world of flavor to explore.

Flanders red and oud bruin are two styles that turn the acidity up even higher. These beers make use of diverse microorganisms, including yeast such as *Brettanomyces* and bacteria like *Lactobacillus*, *Pediococcus*, and *Acetobacter*. Both styles ferment over long periods of time. The results are highly sour, even vinegary, and frequently feature prune, plum, and balsamic notes. A "Desert Island Dish" for me would be a glass of Duchesse de Bourgogne and the smelliest of washed-rind cheeses, perhaps a ripe Époisses—the sourness, sharpness, and huge flavor of the beer is powerful enough to hold its own against the stinky, gooey, fatty cheese… And yes, I'm happy to enjoy that pungent meal on my own.

SOUR GERMAN STYLES

While Belgian sour beers have grown enormously in popularity over the last few decades, it was only a few years ago that German sour styles, such as gose and Berliner weisse, were considered at risk of extinction by some industry observers.

Hurrah, then, for experimental brewers who were getting bored of hops. Both goses and Berliner weisses are examples of "kettle sours," made quickly with *Lactobacillus* bacteria that's added directly to the brew kettle. This technique means they're easier and faster to brew than traditionally soured, mixed- or spontaneous-fermentation beers—and therefore have become a fast favorite of modern brewers.

Goses date back hundreds, if not thousands, of years, and are usually brewed with wheat, salt, and coriander seed. Zesty and saline, goses are ridiculously refreshing, especially on a hot summer's day.

At Hop Burns & Black, we stocked our very first gose from South Carolina's Westbrook Brewing Co when it arrived in the UK in 2015. Now, you'll find hundreds of gose varieties in bottle-shop fridges around the world. Most are low in alcohol and lightly tart and spritzy (and surprisingly ideal for converting a non-beer-lover to the wonderful world of beer), although US brewers especially have been known to turn up the tartness to incredible heights. (My stomach lining still hasn't quite recovered from the insane sourness of Free Will's Key Lime Mojito Sour on a visit to Manhattan beer store Top Hops a couple of years back.)

Berliner weisses are similarly light and refreshing, though they dial up citrus flavors in lieu of salt and spices. These wheat-based beers also date back hundreds of years—Napoleon Bonaparte was reportedly a fan.

In Germany, you'll often be asked if you want your Berliner weisse served with syrup—typically raspberry or bright-green woodruff—although this trend doesn't seem to have followed the beer style out of the country. Instead, both Berliner weisses and goses now incorporate nearly every flavor under the sun, from mushrooms (Wild Beer Co's Breakfast of Champignons) to seaweed (Kereru Brewing's Karengose) and even gin and tonics (Anderson Valley's G&T Gose).

SAISON

The saison style originated in Wallonia—the southern, French-speaking region of Belgium—sometime during the 1700s. As with lambics and gueuzes, brewers took cues from nature to develop this distinct style of beer. Typically, saisons were brewed during the cooler months and kept for seasonal workers to enjoy during the summer, when it was too hot to brew. In order to make it through to summertime, these beers were heavily dosed

with hops to help preserve them. Spices and botanicals, such as coriander seed, orange peel, and peppercorns, provided additional aromatics.

Today, saisons are brewed all over the world. The style encompasses a wide range of characteristics: saisons can be fragrantly hopped, light and biscuity, dry and zesty, or naturally sour. Saisons often act as a showcase for local and seasonal ingredients as well, and may be fermented with fruits, spices, and herbs. But what unites saisons is their yeast. A classic saison yeast (every brewery will have their own favorite or house strain) produces spicy, slightly sweet, peppery, and earthy notes, with fruity, citrusy esters. It's this that helps give saisons their wonderful complexity.

Bière de garde ("beer for keeping") is essentially the French version of a saison—usually slightly sweeter, darker, and maltier than its Belgian counterparts.

A SENSE OF PLACE—BURNING SKY BREWERY, SUSSEX

From Jester King and Allagash in the United States and Burning Sky and Mills Brewing in the UK to 8 Wired and La Sirène in New Zealand and Australia, sour styles and saisons have been embraced by a new generation of breweries around the world.

Burning Sky is firmly rooted in the beautiful English village of Firle, East Sussex (see photograph opposite), and its location is reflected and celebrated in the beers it produces. Its seasonally made saisons, for instance, include ingredients such as nettles, elderflowers, and rosehips foraged from the local fields and hedgerows. While Burning Sky makes equally delicious pale ales and IPAs, it's best known for saisons and sours, and it's clear that these styles most excite founder and head brewer Mark Tranter (above right).

"I love the unpredictable nature of these beers," he says. "The broadness of the styles. The contradictory lightness, yet fullness of flavor and body. The spritzy, refreshing nature, the theater of it all. Just everything—they are the wines of the beer world."

ESSENTIAL BURNING SKY BEERS

• Saison L'Automne: Burning Sky releases four seasonal saisons every year, with each version differing slightly from the last to reflect that season's unique characteristics. All are great, but we especially love L'Automne, as it conjures up the beauty of Firle in the fall (autumn)—golden light, long shadows, hedgerows laden with rosehips against a deep blue sky.
• Cuvée: An annual blend of aged saison from Burning Sky's barriques (small oak wine barrels) blended with Belgian lambic. Light, tart, and incredible with food.

MARK'S PERFECT PAIRING

"One of my most memorable food and beer moments was in a remote restaurant somewhere in Belgium— I couldn't even tell you where it was—with my friend, brewer Eddie Gadd, a bottle of gueuze, and the best smoked salmon with dill and lemon. Seriously good! At home, it's a simple affair—just some good English cheese, our Saison Provision, and the fresh air."

FOOD PAIRINGS

For the beer-focused cook, sours and saisons offer a wealth of potential pairings. They can be spritzy, tart, and refreshing—ideal for seafood—or big and barrel-aged, perfect alongside roasted meats and aged cheeses. Flip through the recipes in this chapter to see how to serve these styles at home, and use the chart below as a guide when crafting your own pairings.

STYLE	CHARACTERISTICS	PAIR WITH
Lambic/gueuze	Tart, funky, wild	Aged cheeses and charcuterie, duck
Oud bruin/Flanders red	Intensely tart, fruity, tannic	Salad with goat's cheese and a fruit vinaigrette, slow-cooked pork shoulder, washed-rind cheese
Berliner weisse	Light, citrusy, gently acidic	Light seafood, Asian cold noodle dishes
Gose	Light, salty, sour	Seared scallops, grilled langoustines, fish tacos
Saison	Dry, effervescent, herbaceous	Roast chicken, cheese, pad Thai
Bière de garde	Dry, malty, amber	Nutty aged cheeses, lamb chops, peppery sausages

CAPRESE SALAD WITH BURRATA

9oz (250g) cherry tomatoes, halved

5–6 tbsps basil-infused olive oil, divided

3–4 large tomatoes (preferably heirloom varieties), cored and thinly sliced

1 burrata, torn into large pieces

Large bunch of fresh basil

Flaky sea salt (such as Maldon) and freshly ground black pepper

SERVES 4 AS A STARTER OR 2 AS A MAIN

Caprese salad is the pure, undiluted taste of late summer and best made when tomatoes are at peak ripeness. Sourcing high-quality ingredients is essential, as this recipe is so simple; by the same token, it's best not to go too far off-piste—don't even think about using potent balsamic vinegar here, for instance. Instead, if you wish to experiment, creamy burrata and basil-infused olive oil take this caprese to the next level (though if you can't find basil-infused olive oil, high-quality extra virgin olive oil works well, too).

PAIR WITH An herbaceous gueuze or sour. Gueuzes hail from Belgium and are prized blends of lambics of varying ages. Funky, sour, and complex, they're extremely versatile when it comes to pairing with food. Alternatively, a sour with bright herbal flavors also fits the bill. Look in particular for those that have been infused with basil.

THREE BEERS TO TRY Chorlton Citra/Basil Extra Sour (UK); Jack's Abby Cucumber Basil Sour (US); Lindemans x Mikkeller SpontanBasil (Belgium)

1 Place the cherry-tomato halves in a small bowl, season to taste with sea salt (I like to use a flaky variety for added crunch), and add 2 tablespoons of the olive oil. Set aside for 10–15 minutes to allow the ingredients to blend and the tomatoes to soften.

2 Arrange the sliced tomatoes on the plates, season to taste with sea salt and black pepper, and drizzle over the remaining 3–4 tablespoons of olive oil.

3 Divide the marinated cherry tomatoes and torn pieces of burrata between the plates.

4 Tear the basil leaves into rough pieces and scatter across the plates. Finish with an extra pinch or two of sea salt and black pepper. Let stand for 10–15 minutes to allow the flavors to infuse before serving.

CITRUS AND SPICE CURED TROUT WITH LEMON RICOTTA PANCAKES

⅔ cup (120g) granulated sugar

½ cup (120g) Kosher salt (preferably Diamond Crystal) or fine sea salt

1 tbsp coriander seeds, crushed

½ tsp freshly ground black pepper

Large bunch of cilantro (fresh coriander)

Large bunch of fresh Thai basil

Trout (or salmon) fillet (about 1lb/450g), skin on

Zest of 2–3 limes

2 lemongrass stalks, finely chopped

FOR THE PANCAKES

Heaping 1 cup (140g) all-purpose (plain) flour

1 tsp baking powder

2 tsps granulated sugar

1½ tsps baking soda (bicarbonate of soda)

Fine sea salt

2 eggs, separated

⅔ cup (150ml) whole milk

Scant 1 cup (200g) ricotta

1 lemon

2 tbsps (30g) unsalted butter

½ cup (125ml) crème fraîche

Freshly ground black pepper

SERVES 4 TO 5 (MAKES APPROXIMATELY 10 PANCAKES)

Curing fish at home is one of those moments of genuine kitchen magic: you start with a simple fillet of fish and, with very little effort, end up with something totally elevated and luxurious. It's a technique I learned from *Bon Appétit* magazine. Here, a trout fillet gets the classic salt-and-sugar cure, with the added benefit of zesty aromatics. If you wish, you can replace the trout with salmon. Instead of blinis, serve the fish on top of ricotta pancakes—these are the fluffiest pancakes I know—and with a swipe of crème fraîche: whether for breakfast, brunch, or dinner, this is perfect everyday decadence.

PAIR WITH A lightly hoppy sour. The acidity of the beer pairs nicely with the fish's citric aromatics and the lemony ricotta pancakes, while the hoppiness serves to temper the several layers of richness in this dish.

THREE BEERS TO TRY Almanac Hoppy Sour Series (US); Buxton x Lervig Trolltunga Gooseberry Sour IPA (UK); Boneface Brewing The Juice Dry Hopped Gose (New Zealand)

1 To prepare the cure for the fish, mix the sugar, Kosher salt, coriander seeds, and black pepper in a bowl. Line a small baking sheet with foil and place half the curing mixture on top, roughly in the shape of the trout fillet. Arrange half the cilantro (fresh coriander) and Thai basil on top of the curing mixture followed by the fish, skin-side down.

2 Sprinkle the lime zest, lemongrass, and remainder of the fresh herbs over the top of the fish. Cover with the remaining curing mixture, ensuring no parts of the fish are exposed. Place a second layer of foil over the first, fold to create a tightly sealed parcel, and place in the refrigerator. Weigh the fish down with a few heavy objects (several bottles of beer will do the trick) and chill for 12 hours. After 12 hours, flip the parcel over and put the heavy objects back on top. Let chill for a further 12 hours. Please note: if the fish fillet is particularly thick, you may wish to let it cure for up to 30 hours.

3 Remove the fish from the refrigerator, rinse off any excess curing mixture, and pat dry with paper towels. Line the baking sheet with a new piece of foil and put a wire rack on top. Place the fish, skin-side down, on the rack and return to the refrigerator, leaving it to air-dry for 8 hours. Using a very sharp knife, gently separate the skin from the fish and discard. Cover the fish with plastic wrap (clingfilm) and keep in the refrigerator for up to three days.

4 To make the batter for the pancakes, mix together the flour, baking powder, sugar, baking soda (bicarbonate of soda), and a pinch of fine sea salt in a medium bowl. In a separate large bowl, whisk together the egg yolks, milk, ricotta, the zest of the whole lemon, and the juice of half the lemon. Add the dry ingredients to the wet ingredients, and stir until just combined (do not overmix).

5 In another bowl, whisk the egg whites with an electric hand mixer for several minutes until they form firm, but not stiff, peaks. Add a large dollop of egg whites to the ricotta mix and stir gently to combine. Add the remainder of the egg whites and fold in with a spatula until incorporated. The pancake batter should be light and airy.

6 Heat a large skillet (frying pan) over medium heat and add enough butter to coat the bottom. When the butter has melted, use a measuring cup or pitcher (jug) to dollop out about ½ cup (125ml) of batter for each pancake (you should be able to cook two or three pancakes in the same skillet, depending on the size). Let the pancakes cook for about 3 minutes, or until the undersides are golden, then gently flip them over with a spatula. Cook for a further 2 minutes, or until the pancakes are cooked through and golden on both sides. Remove the pancakes from the skillet and repeat, adding more butter if necessary, until you have used all the batter. (You can keep the cooked pancakes warm in the oven on a low heat on a foil-covered tray.)

7 To finish, use a sharp knife to slice the fish thinly on a bias. Top each pancake with a swipe of crème fraîche and several slices of fish. Season to taste with more sea salt and black pepper, and squeeze over the remaining lemon half.

SEARED SCALLOPS WITH SAMPHIRE AND HAZELNUT CRUMBLE

¼ cup (30g) whole blanched hazelnuts

6 large scallops

3½ oz (100g) samphire

2 tbsps (30g) unsalted butter

½ lemon

Fine sea salt and freshly ground black pepper

4 tbsps micro herbs (such as basil, sorrel, and mint), to garnish

SERVES 2

In this springy starter, sweet, tender scallops are served on top of a bed of samphire. If you're not familiar with samphire, think of it as a cousin to asparagus—small, knobbly, and always an excellent companion to seafood (Jen likes it for its salty snap). A spritz of lemon juice and garnish of micro herbs add additional brightness and the looks to match: this is the kind of dish that goes down well at dinner parties.

PAIR WITH A citrusy gose. Goses originally hail from Leipzig, Germany, and are known both for their sourness and salinity. Here, they bring a refreshing tartness that won't overwhelm the dish.

THREE BEERS TO TRY Kereru Brewing Karengose Salty Seaweed Ale (New Zealand); Two Roads x Evil Twin Geyser Gose (US); Wild Beer Co Sleeping Lemons Gose (UK)

1 Heat a small skillet (frying pan) over medium-high heat. Add the hazelnuts and toast, tossing occasionally, for 5–6 minutes or until they are fragrant and golden brown. Remove from the heat and let cool for a few minutes. Transfer the hazelnuts to a food processor and pulse until finely chopped. Set aside.

2 Rinse the scallops (discarding the roe, if you prefer) and pat dry with paper towels. Season both sides of the scallops with sea salt and black pepper.

3 Bring a medium saucepan of water to a boil and add a pinch or two of sea salt (keep in mind that the samphire may be quite salty already). Pick through the samphire, discarding any woody pieces, and add to the boiling water. Cook for 2 minutes, or until the samphire is tender but still has some bite. Drain the samphire, divide between two plates, and grind over some black pepper, to taste.

4 Heat the butter in the skillet over high heat. Once the butter has melted and started to foam, add the scallops and cook for 1½ minutes. Flip the scallops over and cook for a further 1½ minutes, then remove from the skillet. The scallops should have a golden crust on both sides, but be tender in the middle. Place three scallops on top of the samphire on each plate.

5 Add the chopped hazelnuts to the browned butter remaining in the skillet, and stir for 30 seconds over low heat. Spoon the hazelnuts over the samphire and scallops.

6 To finish, squeeze the lemon half over both plates and top with more freshly ground black pepper. Garnish with the micro herbs.

CHEDDAR AND CHIVE BISCUITS WITH TOMATO JAM

Scant 3 cups (350g) all-purpose (plain) flour, plus extra for dusting

½ tsp fine sea salt

2½ tsps baking powder

1 tsp baking soda (bicarbonate of soda)

1½ tsps granulated sugar

1 stick (115g) butter, frozen

1¼ cups (125g) grated sharp (mature) Cheddar cheese

Large bunch of fresh chives, finely chopped

1 cup (250ml) chilled buttermilk, plus an extra 1–2 tbsps if needed

2 tbsps (30g) unsalted butter, melted

FOR THE TOMATO JAM

1½ tbsps olive oil

1 small red onion, thinly sliced

1 large garlic clove, finely chopped

1 tsp cumin seeds

¾ tsp red pepper (dried chili) flakes

1lb (450g) plum tomatoes, cored and chopped

2 tbsps light brown sugar

1 tbsp red wine vinegar

½ tsp fine sea salt

Freshly ground black pepper

I don't have much of a sweet tooth, so most of my baking projects fall on the savory side of the spectrum. Cheesy, Southern-style biscuits (similar to scones in the UK) are a favorite of mine: flaky but still tender, they're irresistible eaten warm from the oven, slathered with not-too-sweet tomato jam. (In fact, they're best enjoyed fresh—bake them when you have a group coming for brunch.) While making biscuits (scones) with frozen butter might sound strange, the technique produces an extra flaky crumb.

PAIR WITH A bready, biscuity saison. Saisons are a food-friendly beer style, as adept at cutting through fat (in this case, cheese and butter) as they are at complementing acidity (the brightness of the tomato jam).

THREE BEERS TO TRY Brasserie Dupont Saison Dupont (Belgium); Brew By Numbers Table Saison—Sorachi Ace & Lemon (UK); Prairie Artisan Ales Prairie Ace (US)

1 To make the tomato jam, heat the olive oil in a saucepan over medium-high heat, add the onion, and stir frequently until softened (about 3–5 minutes). Add the garlic and stir for a further minute. Add the cumin seeds and pepper (chili) flakes, and stir for 1–2 minutes, or until the spices are fragrant.

2 Add the tomatoes, sugar, vinegar, and sea salt to the saucepan, and stir. Season with a few good grinds of black pepper. Bring the mixture to a boil, then reduce the heat to low and let simmer for approximately 1 hour, stirring occasionally until it has thickened and reduced. Season to taste, remove from the heat, and set aside to cool.

3 Meanwhile, prepare the biscuits (scones). Preheat the oven to 425°F/220°C/Gas 7 and line a baking sheet with parchment (baking) paper.

4 Mix the flour, salt, baking powder, baking soda (bicarbonate of soda), and sugar in a large bowl. Remove the butter from the freezer and, working quickly so it doesn't warm up and soften, grate it finely into the flour mixture, stirring occasionally to prevent clumps.

5 Add the Cheddar cheese and chives, and mix gently to combine. Form a well in the center of the dry mixture and pour in the buttermilk. Stir to form a dough that is slightly sticky and pulls away from the sides of the bowl in one mass. If the dough appears a little dry, or if there are still floury bits at the bottom of the bowl, stir in 1–2 more tablespoons of buttermilk.

6 Lightly dust a work surface, your hands, and a rolling pin with flour. Turn the dough out onto the work surface and roll to form a rectangle measuring approximately 10 x 6 inches (25 x 15cm) and 1 inch (2.5cm) thick.

7 Lightly flour a biscuit cutter (if you don't have one of these, a ½-cup measure also works well) and press straight down into the dough; it should make a gentle sighing sound. Place the biscuit on the prepared baking sheet and repeat, leaving 1 inch (2.5cm) between each biscuit. You may need to re-roll the scraps of dough once or twice; if you have more biscuits than will fit comfortably on the baking sheet, prepare a second one. Brush the tops of the biscuits with the melted butter just before they go in the oven.

8 Bake the biscuits for approximately 12–14 minutes, or until they have risen and are deep golden on top. (If your oven has hot spots, rotate the baking sheet halfway through the cooking time.) Remove the biscuits from the oven and transfer to a cooling rack. Let cool for 5 minutes before cutting each biscuit in half and adding a dollop of tomato jam. The biscuits are best eaten fresh from the oven, but will keep covered in the refrigerator for several days. If covered, the jam last for up to five days in the refrigerator.

SPRING ORECCHIETTE

1 stick (115g) unsalted butter, divided

1 cup (100g) blanched almonds, roughly chopped

1 tsp dried culinary lavender, plus extra to garnish

1lb (450g) dried orecchiette

8oz (225g) asparagus (woody ends removed), sliced into 1-inch (2.5cm) pieces

1⅓ cups (200g) shelled peas

Small bunch of ramps (wild garlic)

4½ oz (125g) goat's cheese, divided

Zest of 1 lemon

Fine sea salt and freshly ground black pepper

Freshly shaved Parmigiano Reggiano, to serve

SERVES 5

Asparagus and peas are both verdant signals of early spring, and their arrival in grocery stores and farmers' markets always fills me with anticipation. So does the appearance of leafy ramps (often referred to as wild garlic)—available for only a few weeks every year, it's the perfect way to infuse your cooking with a piquant, allium-y bite. All three share the spotlight in this spring pasta dish, alongside crumbly goat's cheese and browned almonds that have been delicately scented with lavender.

PAIR WITH A light, citrusy kettle sour. Beers made using the kettle-souring technique have been inoculated with *lactobacillus*: the same bacteria that's found in yogurt and other dairy products. Kettle sours are typically light on the palate and have a bright tartness, which means they won't overwhelm the delicate flavors in this dish.

THREE BEERS TO TRY Cloudwater Bergamot Sour (UK); North End Brewery Salt and Wood Become the Ocean Gose (New Zealand); Westbrook Gose (US)

1 Add 7 tablespoons (100g) of the butter to a small skillet (frying pan) and place over medium-high heat. Once the butter has just melted, add the chopped almonds. Cook for about 3 minutes, stirring frequently, or until the almonds are toasted. The butter will foam up as it begins to brown—watch carefully, as it can go from browned to burned very quickly. When the butter has darkened and smells nutty and toasty, remove the skillet from the heat and pour the buttery almonds into a bowl to cool. Add the lavender to the bowl, stir, and set aside.

2 Bring a large saucepan of well-salted water to a gentle boil, add the pasta, and cook for about 10 minutes or until al dente.

3 While the pasta is cooking, melt the remaining butter in a large skillet over medium-high heat. Add the asparagus and peas, and cook for 3–5 minutes, or until the vegetables are bright green and just tender. Roughly tear the ramps (wild garlic) leaves and add to the skillet, stirring until they begin to wilt (about 30 seconds). Remove the skillet from the heat.

4 Drain the pasta, reserving approximately ½ cup (125ml) of the cooking water. Return the pasta to the pan, tip in the asparagus, pea, and ramps mix, and toss to combine.

5 Strain the lavender-flavored butter from the almonds into the pasta, then add half the reserved cooking water and crumble in three-quarters of the goat's cheese. Stir until a light sauce forms, adding small amounts of additional cooking water if necessary to help the sauce bind. Season to taste.

6 Divide the pasta among the plates, crumbling over the remaining goat's cheese and adding the lemon zest, toasted almonds, extra lavender, and a generous amount of black pepper. Sprinkle with the grated Parmigiano Reggiano and serve immediately.

WHOLE ROASTED SALMON WITH ORANGE, FENNEL, AND VERMOUTH

3 large fennel bulbs, thinly sliced

1 large onion, thinly sliced

Small bunch of fresh flat-leaf parsley, divided

Small bunch of fresh tarragon leaves, divided

Small bunch of fresh dill, divided

2 oranges

Whole salmon (about 5½lb/2.5kg), cleaned and scaled

½ cup (125ml) olive oil

½ cup (125ml) white vermouth

Fine sea salt and freshly ground black pepper

SERVES 8 TO 10

Roasting a whole salmon is the makings of an excellent dinner party. Both a spectacle and a participatory exercise, it's a dish that encourages interaction and the licking of fingers. This version gets a Provençal treatment, with fennel, fresh herbs, oranges, and vermouth. Serve at the height of summer, preferably outdoors, and maybe with a seasonal salad on the side.

PAIR WITH An orange sour or saison. Both light, spritzy sours and slightly richer saisons go well with this dish's acidity and herbaceousness—particularly beers that, like the salmon, are infused with orange flavors and have a touch of sweetness.

THREE BEERS TO TRY Anderson Valley Blood Orange Gose (US); Elusive x Hop Burns & Black Bright Future (UK); Upslope Brewing Blood Orange Saison (US)

1 Preheat the oven to 350°F/180°C/Gas 4. Line the largest roasting pan you have with heavy-duty foil, add the sliced fennel and onion, and season to taste with sea salt and black pepper.

2 Take half the parsley, tarragon, and dill, chop finely, and add to a small bowl. Zest the oranges (preferably with a Microplane grater, so you don't remove the bitter pith) and add the zest to the chopped herbs. Set the bowl aside and reserve the two oranges.

3 To prepare the salmon, pat the inside and outside dry with paper towels. Ensure the salmon has been fully scaled (if there are any scales remaining, scrape them away with the back of a knife, moving against the grain of the scales). Use a sharp knife to make five ½-inch (1cm) slits at an angle in the side of the salmon. Season the salmon very generously inside and out with sea salt. Add more salt, as well as some chopped herb and orange zest mixture, to each slit. Flip the salmon over and repeat the slitting and seasoning steps on the other side.

4 Transfer the salmon to the roasting pan and place on top of the sliced fennel and onion. Slice the reserved oranges into wheels and place the slices, plus the remaining whole herbs, inside the cavity of the salmon. Pour the olive oil and vermouth over the salmon. Place a second piece of heavy-duty foil on top of the salmon and crimp to make a parcel and seal the fish and vegetables inside.

5 Roast the salmon in the oven for 50 minutes to 1 hour, or until a knife inserted in the flesh near the head feels warm to the touch and the flesh appears flaky. Once the salmon is cooked through, serve with the sliced fennel and onion, seasoning to taste.

"FREE-FROM" BEERS BY JEN FERGUSON

There was a time, not long ago, when the choices were dire if you wanted to drink beer without alcohol or gluten. Thankfully, science and innovation have come to the rescue. Today, the options are wide-ranging, and the quality often so high that you'd struggle to tell "free-from" and regular beer apart.

NO- AND LOW-ALCOHOL BEERS

The popularity of no- and low-alcohol beers has increased exponentially in recent years. Our shops alone saw sales jump 150 percent in the space of a year. Reasons for the increase are many and varied. The wellness movement, for example, has driven people to focus more on health than in the past, and statistics show Millennials are less likely to drink alcohol than older generations.

A new breed of brewers dedicated to no- and low-ABV beers has responded to the growing demand. The likes of Small Beer Brew Co, Nirvana, and Big Drop in the UK, alongside Bravus Brewing Co and WellBeing in the US, are all making waves. Additionally, many top breweries have added no- or low-alcohol beers to their ranges.

Mass-market no- and low-alcohol offerings have often been achieved by de-alcoholizing the beer through a process called reverse osmosis, which strips the alcohol (and often flavor) from the beer. The methods small-batch breweries use to produce so-called "small beer," however, can be much more complex—involving slower fermentation times, smart use of hops and various techniques, including arrested fermentation and distillation—and are designed to retain character.

Small Beer head brewer Felix James says, "Instead of the traditional brewer's efficiency—achieving as much alcohol as possible out of the raw materials you put in—we aim for flavor efficiency. How can we achieve the best tasting beer while keeping the alcohol levels in check? Brewing great-tasting beers at a low ABV isn't easy—it involves a level of accuracy and attention to detail which isn't nearly as critical when brewing bigger beers that will masque small variations in the process."

GLUTEN-FREE BEERS

In the last few years, coinciding with a rise in the number of people moving to a gluten-free lifestyle, gluten-free brewing processes have advanced considerably. The majority of gluten-free craft beers now use a process known as de-glutenizing. This technique takes beer brewed the traditional way, using barley (a grain that is not gluten-free), but adds an enzyme to break up the gluten protein strands. De-glutenizing brings the beer's gluten level to below 20 parts per million (ppm), the legal requirement for foods to be labeled "gluten-free" in many countries.

However, these beers may not be suitable for true celiacs—those who cannot tolerate any gluten, rather than those who are gluten-sensitive or who merely want to avoid gluten. Luckily, there are talented brewers using no-gluten grains to make wonderful beers. British brewery Burnt Mill is renowned for its Steel Cut Pale Ale, an exceptional beer made entirely from gluten-free grains such as buckwheat, maize, and sorghum. Head brewer Sophie de Ronde learned she was not just gluten-intolerant but actually allergic to barley and wheat in 2016. Her allergy is such that even gluten-removed beers are too potent. With Steel Cut, she decided to brew a beer she and many others could enjoy—conveniently at the same time demand for gluten-free beers was rising.

"Steel Cut is a challenging beer," says de Ronde. "We have to make sure that every ounce of grain is removed from the kit before we brew it; it's also hard to get consistent yields from. However, it's turned out to be a great pale ale that most people can enjoy—and it just happens to be gluten-free."

THREE NO- AND LOW-ALCOHOL BEERS TO TRY

Mikkeller Drinkin' In The Sun Pale Ale, 0.3% (Denmark)
Small Beer Dark Lager, 1% (UK)
WellBeing Heavenly Body Golden Wheat, 0.5% (US)

THREE GLUTEN-FREE BEERS TO TRY

Burnt Mill Steel Cut Pale Ale (UK)
New Belgium Glütiny Pale Ale (US)
Magic Rock Saucery Session IPA (UK)

SOBA NOODLES WITH EDAMAME, MISO, AND FRESH HERBS

2 tbsps sesame seeds

3 tbsps white miso paste

2 tbsps toasted sesame oil

2 tbsps mirin

2 tbsps soy sauce

1 tsp chili garlic sauce

1 tsp Chinkiang vinegar (Chinese black rice vinegar)

Juice of 1 lemon

1-inch (2.5cm) piece of fresh ginger, peeled and finely chopped

14oz (400g) green tea soba noodles (or use regular noodles)

10½ oz (300g) edamame, shelled and cooked

½ cucumber, very finely sliced

Small bunch of fresh mint, roughly chopped

Small bunch of cilantro (fresh coriander), roughly chopped

Small bunch of scallions (spring onions), green parts thinly sliced and white parts discarded

Fine sea salt

SERVES 4

Cold noodles were made for sultry summer days. Topped with refreshing cucumber slices, handfuls of fresh herbs, and a piquant miso sauce, these Japanese-inflected soba noodles could be classed as a hearty salad or a light main dish—either way, they're best enjoyed when the weather's at its warmest. This is one of Jen's favorite recipes in the book—she fell in love with soba on her first visit to Japan in 2009. Even at the most modest establishments, they're simple perfection and a much-needed respite on a sweltering summer day in Tokyo.

PAIR WITH A lactic Berliner weisse. Light, tart German wheat beers that are often flavored with fruit syrups, Berliner weisses are frequently fermented with *Lactobacillus*, which can lend the style a dairy-like tang. Find a cucumber-flavored Berliner weisse and you've really perfected this pairing.

THREE BEERS TO TRY 8 Wired Cucumber Hippy Berliner (New Zealand); Jackie O's Cucumber Ginger Berliner Weisse (US); Oakshire Brewing Sun Made Cucumber (US)

1 Toast the sesame seeds in a small skillet (frying pan) over medium heat, tossing frequently, for 2–3 minutes, or until the seeds are golden brown. Watch attentively, as they can burn very quickly. Transfer to a small bowl and set aside.

2 To make the miso sauce, whisk the miso paste, sesame oil, mirin, soy sauce, chili garlic sauce, Chinkiang vinegar, lemon juice, and ginger in a bowl.

3 Bring a saucepan of salted water to a boil over high heat. Add the soba noodles and cook according to the packet directions or until al dente (approximately 4 minutes).

4 Drain the noodles and rinse in cold water, then drain again, so they are at room temperature.

5 Place the noodles in a large serving bowl and add the edamame and miso sauce. Toss with tongs until the noodles are well coated in the sauce.

6 Top the noodles with the cucumber, mint, cilantro (fresh coriander), and scallions (spring onions), and toss gently. Sprinkle over the toasted sesame seeds and serve.

1¼ tbsps fine sea salt

1 tsp freshly ground black pepper

1 tbsp light brown sugar

1 tbsp coriander seeds, roughly ground

1 tbsp cumin seeds, roughly ground

Roasting (whole) chicken (about 2½–3lb/1.1–1.3kg)

FOR THE HARISSA GLAZE

3 tbsps thick harissa paste (preferably the variety that comes in a tube)

3 tbsps olive oil

2 tbsps clear honey

Zest and juice of 1 lemon

3 garlic cloves, finely chopped

FOR THE PINE NUT COUSCOUS

2 tbsps olive oil, divided

1¾ cups (300g) couscous

1½ cups (350ml) chicken stock

3½ tbsps (50g) unsalted butter

¾ cup (100g) pine nuts

3½ oz (100g) feta

Small bunch of fresh parsley, finely chopped

Zest and juice of 1 lemon

Fine sea salt and freshly ground black pepper

SERVES 4

Roast chicken is one of the simplest and most soul-satisfying dishes out there, but there are a few tweaks you can make to produce an especially tasty bird. Try salting the chicken generously and leaving it to air-dry in the refrigerator overnight for extra juicy, flavorful meat. Spatchcocking, or butterflying, the chicken helps, too—removing the backbone and pressing the chicken flat ensures it cooks faster and more evenly.

PAIR WITH A dry, zesty saison. The chicken's complex, spice-driven flavors need a beer that can hold its own, so look for a saison with a solid body and aromatic esters. Lighter, tarter saisons need not apply here.

THREE BEERS TO TRY Partizan Lemon and Thyme Saison (UK); Pasteur Street Brewing Saigon Saison (Vietnam); Tired Hands SaisonHands (US)

1 Prepare the dry brine mixture the night before you plan to roast the chicken. Add the Kosher salt, black pepper, sugar, coriander seeds, and cumin seeds to a small bowl and mix to combine.

2 To spatchcock the chicken, use kitchen shears or a very sharp knife to carefully slice all the way along one side of the chicken's spine, and then along the other. Remove the spine and discard (or save it for making stock later). Flip the chicken over so it is breast-side up and the legs are splayed to the sides, then press on the breastbone with the heel of your hand to flatten, until you hear a cracking sound.

3 Rub the chicken all over with the dry brine mixture. Line a baking sheet with foil and put a wire rack on top. Place the chicken, breast-side up, on the rack and chill, uncovered, overnight (or for up to 24 hours) in the refrigerator.

4 The next day, take the chicken out of the fridge. Preheat the oven to 400°F/200°C/Gas 6.

5 To prepare the glaze, mix the harissa paste, olive oil, honey, lemon zest and juice, and garlic in a small bowl. Rub the paste all over the chicken, including under the skin.

6 Roast the chicken in the oven for 20 minutes, covering with foil if it starts to darken. After 20 minutes, reduce the heat to 350°F/180°C/Gas 4 and cook for a further 15 minutes, or until a meat thermometer in a thick part of the thigh registers 167°F (75°C).

7 While the chicken is roasting, for the couscous heat 1 tablespoon of the olive oil over medium-high heat in a small saucepan. Add the couscous and toast lightly, stirring constantly, for 2–3 minutes, or until it is slightly darkened. Pour in the stock and bring to a boil. Cover immediately, remove from the heat, and let stand for 15 minutes.

8 Meanwhile, melt the butter in a small skillet (frying pan) and add the pine nuts. Cook for 2–3 minutes, stirring frequently, until the butter foams up and browns and the pine nuts are toasted and smell nutty. Remove from the heat and set aside.

9 Use a fork to fluff up the couscous in the saucepan. Crumble in the feta and add the pine nut mixture, parsley, remaining tablespoon of olive oil, and lemon zest and juice. Season to taste with sea salt and black pepper, then mix gently to combine.

10 Let the chicken rest for 5–10 minutes before carving, then serve with the couscous.

CONFIT SWEET POTATOES WITH CRUNCHY CHICKPEAS AND TAHINI

2 medium sweet potatoes (about 1¼ lb/600g), scrubbed clean and cut into ½-inch (1cm) rounds

2 cups (500ml) olive oil, plus extra if using multiple roasting pans

Fine sea salt and freshly ground black pepper

Small bunch of parsley, roughly chopped, and zest of 1 lime, to garnish

Greens, to serve (optional)

FOR THE CRUNCHY CHICKPEAS

1 14oz (400g) can chickpeas, drained and rinsed

2 tbsps olive oil

1 tsp ground cumin

½ tsp ground cinnamon

½ tsp cayenne pepper

½ tsp fine sea salt

FOR THE TAHINI SAUCE

½ cup (125ml) tahini, whisked before measuring

½ cup (125ml) ice-cold water

Juice of ½ lemon

1 garlic clove, finely chopped

¼ tsp fine sea salt

SERVES 4 AS A STARTER OR 2 AS A MAIN

Confiting—a decadent technique that uses fat as a cooking medium instead of water—is often reserved for duck, but it works just as well for vegetables. Here, sweet potatoes are immersed in simmering olive oil and slow-cooked before being quickly caramelized on the stovetop. Roasted chickpeas add crunch and spice, tahini sauce brings nuttiness and a touch of acidity, and lime zest and parsley tie the whole dish together. Bold flavors make this a fitting choice for veggies and vegans, those going gluten-free, or simply carnivores after a meal sans meat.

PAIR WITH A funky saison or complex gueuze. Both styles work with the heft of the confit sweet potatoes and creamy tahini sauce, while mirroring the dish's citric acidity.

THREE BEERS TO TRY Brasserie de la Senne Bruxellensis (Belgium); Burning Sky Saison à la Provision (UK); Cellar West Artisan Ales Make Hay (US)

1 Preheat the oven to 425°F/220°C/Gas 7 and line a baking sheet with parchment (baking) paper.

2 First, make the crunchy chickpeas. Pat the chickpeas dry with paper towels and add to a medium bowl with the olive oil, spices, and sea salt. Stir to coat the chickpeas evenly, then pour onto the lined baking sheet in a single layer and bake for 10 minutes. Remove from the oven, stir, and bake for a further 10 minutes (handle the chickpeas carefully, as several may burst in the heat). They should be darkened and crisp, but still just slightly tender in the center—roast for a further 5–7 minutes if you want the chickpeas extra crispy. Set aside and let cool.

3 Lower the oven temperature to 275°F/140°C/Gas 1. Add the sweet potato slices to a roasting pan in a single layer. Season to taste with sea salt and black pepper. Pour over the olive oil, so it just covers the slices. (If the pan isn't big enough to hold all the sweet potato, divide between two pans and increase the amount of olive oil so the slices are fully immersed in both pans.) Roast for 1 hour, or until the sweet potatoes are very tender but still hold their shape. The oil should simmer gently throughout the cooking process; if it bubbles more rapidly, turn the heat down by 10–20°.

4 Meanwhile, to make the tahini sauce, add the tahini to a bowl and slowly incorporate the ice-cold water, whisking constantly. It may look clotted at first, but continue to whisk rapidly and it should fully emulsify into a smooth, whipped sauce. Whisk in the lemon juice, garlic, and sea salt. Set aside.

5 When the sweet potato slices are cooked, take the tray from the oven and let cool for several minutes. Remove the slices from the oil with a slotted spoon or spider strainer and let cool slightly on a baking paper-lined plate. Reserve several tablespoons of the cooking oil (and safely dispose of the remainder once cooled).

6 Heat a large skillet (frying pan) over medium-high heat and add just enough of the reserved oil to coat the base. Gently add the sweet potato slices in a single layer—you will probably have to do this in two batches—and cook for 2 minutes, or until the slices are caramelized on the bottom. Flip the slices over and cook for a further 1–2 minutes. Set aside and repeat for the second batch, adding more oil to the skillet if the slices start to stick.

7 To serve, divide the sweet potato slices between the plates and drizzle over the tahini sauce. Top each plate with a large handful of crunchy chickpeas. Garnish with the chopped parsley and lime zest (plus a twist of black pepper, if desired). To add an additional component to the dish, serve on a bed of greens.

LAMB BURGERS WITH QUICK PICKLES AND WHIPPED FETA

2¼ lb (1kg) 20%-fat ground (minced) lamb

¾ cup (100g) toasted pine nuts (see Savory Pesto Tomato Muffins, Step 2, page 56, for guidance on toasting)

1 tsp ground cinnamon

1 tbsp ground cumin

1 tsp chili powder

1 tsp paprika

1 egg

1½ tbsps tomato paste (purée)

2 echalion (banana) shallots, finely chopped

1½ tsps fine sea salt

1 tsp freshly ground black pepper

Olive oil, for frying

6 burger buns or large, whole-wheat (wholemeal) pitas

Large bunch of mint, chopped

You don't need an outdoor grill to make these vaguely Levantine lamb burgers, which are flecked with pine nuts and generously seasoned with an array of spices. Likewise, you don't need any special equipment to make your own pickles at home: these quick-pickled carrot and cucumber slices require just 10 minutes of active prep time (and taste far better than anything you can buy at the grocery store). Finish the burgers with a dollop of whipped feta and a fistful of mint leaves for an ideal balance of freshness, saltiness, and acidity, then serve in burger buns or pitas. (If you use pitas, look for large, fluffy ones that won't fall apart once the burgers and toppings are added.)

PAIR WITH A hoppy saison. Many saisons have a flavor profile that leans toward funk, which works well with the gamy intensity of lamb. A good dose of hoppy bitterness also helps cut through fat and counterbalances the richness of the burgers.

THREE BEERS TO TRY Funkwerks Nelson Sauvin Saison (US); Jolly Pumpkin Bam Bière (US); La Sirène Urban Pale (Australia)

1 To make the quick pickles, bring the vinegars, water, sugar, bay leaf, spices, and sea salt to a boil in a small saucepan.

2 Add the sliced cucumber and carrot to a sterilized glass jar with a sealable lid.

3 Remove the saucepan from the heat and carefully pour the pickling mixture over the carrots and cucumbers. Let sit on the countertop until the jar reaches room temperature, then seal and chill in the refrigerator for at least 2 hours.

4 To prepare the lamb burgers, add the lamb, toasted pine nuts, spices, egg, tomato paste (purée), shallots, Kosher salt, and black pepper to a large, nonreactive bowl. Mix with your hands until well combined. Cover with plastic wrap (clingfilm) and chill for 1–2 hours to let the flavors blend.

5 Remove the lamb from the refrigerator at least 30 minutes before cooking to bring it to room temperature.

⅓ cup (75ml) white wine
vinegar

⅓ cup (75ml) apple cider
vinegar

Scant ¼ cup (50ml) water

1½ tbsps granulated sugar

1 fresh bay leaf

1½ tsps anise seed

½ tbsp whole black
peppercorns

½ tbsp mustard seeds

½ tbsp coriander seeds

½ tbsp fine sea salt

½ cucumber, very thinly
sliced

1 medium carrot, peeled
and very thinly sliced

FOR THE WHIPPED FETA

7oz (200g) feta, at room
temperature

⅔ cup (150g) Greek yogurt
or labneh, at room
temperature

2 tbsps fresh mint, roughly
chopped

Juice of ½ lime

2 tbsps extra virgin olive
oil

½ tsp ground sumac

1 garlic clove, finely
chopped

Freshly ground black
pepper

SERVES 6

6 Meanwhile, to make the whipped feta, combine all the ingredients in a food processor. Mix on high speed, pausing occasionally to scrape down the sides of the bowl with a spatula, for 2–3 minutes, or until the mixture is smooth, thick, and slightly glossy. Set aside.

7 Shape the lamb mixture into six equally sized burger patties. Heat two large skillets (frying pans) over medium heat and add just enough olive oil to coat the bases. (If you prefer, you can use just one skillet and cook the patties in batches.) Cook the patties for approximately 4 minutes, or until well browned on the bottom, then flip them over and cook for a further 4 minutes, or until browned on the other side. Remove from the heat and set aside for 5 minutes.

8 If you are using burger buns, slice them in half and toast in a dry skillet, cut sides down, for 1–2 minutes, or until golden (you may need to do this in several batches). If you are using pitas, toast each pita in a toaster or under a broiler (grill) for 1–2 minutes. Use kitchen shears or a sharp knife to slice one-third off the top of each pita. Gently open each pita like a pocket and line the bottom with the piece you removed—this will help catch any drips as you eat.

9 To serve, put together each burger by swiping a generous amount of whipped feta on the bottom half of the bun or inside the pita. Top with a small handful of chopped mint, followed by the patty. Add a few pickles (don't worry if any of the spices have stuck—these add a nice crunch and flavor) and serve.

VANILLA PANNA COTTA WITH RHUBARB COMPOTE

2 sheets (leaves) gelatin

1¼ cups (300ml) heavy (double) cream

⅔ cup (150ml) whole milk

½ cup (95g) granulated sugar

1 tsp vanilla paste or vanilla extract

2 Amaretti cookies or ginger snaps, roughly crumbled, to serve

FOR THE RHUBARB COMPOTE

12oz (350g) rhubarb, trimmed and sliced into ½-inch (1cm) pieces

Juice of 1 lemon

¾ cup (140g) granulated sugar

½ tsp ground cardamom

SERVES 4

Think of this as a remix of rhubarb and custard, that most traditional of British springtime desserts. I love custard, but in warmer weather fridge-chilled panna cotta hits the right spot. Lightly creamy and slightly wobbly, it's the picture of simplicity served alone, but even better with a fruit complement—rhubarb compote, in this case, which brings piquancy, tartness, and its unmissable hue to the table.

PAIR WITH A fruity sour. Young, fruit-led lambics work better here than older, funkier numbers. You can't go wrong with a beer with residual sweetness, ripe flavors, and a deep red hue.

THREE BEERS TO TRY Great Divide Strawberry Rhubarb Sour Ale (US); Grimm Cherry Raspberry Pop! (US); Omnipollo Nautilus (Sweden)

1 Soften the gelatin sheets (leaves) in a small bowl of cold water while you prepare the panna cotta.

2 Heat the cream, milk, and sugar in a saucepan over medium heat until the mixture is simmering. Remove the pan from the stovetop. Squeeze any water out of the gelatin sheets, add the sheets to the cream mixture, and stir until completely dissolved. Add the vanilla paste or vanilla extract and stir to combine.

3 Pour the panna-cotta mixture into four ramekins and let stand on the countertop to cool to room temperature. Place the ramekins in the refrigerator to chill for a minimum of 3–4 hours, or preferably overnight.

4 To make the rhubarb compote, cook the rhubarb, lemon juice, sugar, and cardamom in a saucepan over medium heat for 10–12 minutes, or until the rhubarb has broken down and the compote has thickened. Set aside and let cool.

5 To serve, flip each ramekin upside down onto a plate; the panna cotta should slide out gently. If not, briefly immerse the base of the ramekin in very hot water to help loosen the panna cotta, and try again. Dollop compote around each panna cotta and top with the crumbled Amaretti cookies or ginger snaps.

PHYLLO TART WITH APRICOT JAM

1¼ cups (300ml) heavy (double) cream

2 egg yolks

Scant ¼ cup (50ml) whole milk

½ tsp almond extract

½ tsp vanilla extract

1 tsp ground cardamom

1 tbsp clear honey, plus extra for drizzling

7–8 sheets of phyllo (filo) pastry, defrosted if frozen

1½ tbsps (20g) butter, melted

7oz (200g) apricot jam

¾ cup (75g) slivered (nibbed) pistachios

SERVES 6

Phyllo (filo) dough is magic. Before I ever experimented with it, I thought those paper-thin tissues of pastry must be terribly delicate and difficult to work with. But that couldn't be further from the truth, and phyllo tarts, both sweet and savory, are now a staple in my kitchen. This version, which is sweetened with apricot jam and honey, scented with almond and cardamom, and made rich with cream, comes together quickly (and brings with it the whiff of a Mediterranean summer).

PAIR WITH A stone fruit sour. Apricot jam is a key element in this dessert and, in a case of like pairing with like, a sweet-tart apricot sour makes an able companion.

THREE BEERS TO TRY Cantillon Fou'Foune (Belgium); Casey Brewing & Blending Fruit Stand Farmhouse Ale (US); The Kernel Bière de Saison Apricot (UK)

1 Preheat the oven to 400°F/200°C/Gas 6. Use a medium-sized baking dish (approximately 7 x 11 inches/18 x 28cm), preferably made from Pyrex or ceramic.

2 Whisk the cream, egg yolks, milk, almond and vanilla extracts, cardamom, and honey in a medium bowl. Set aside.

3 Take 1 sheet of phyllo (filo) pastry and line the baking dish, ensuring it covers the sides evenly. Brush lightly with the melted butter, reserving some for later.

4 Place a second sheet of pastry on the counter and position it so the longest side is facing you. Fold the sheet in half from bottom to top. Use a knife to spread a thin layer of apricot jam over the top half of the folded pastry. Sprinkle over enough pistachios to cover the pastry lightly (reserving some to use as a garnish). Fold the sheet in half again, from the bottom, so the jam and pistachio layer is sealed in—you should now have one long strip of folded-over pastry. Roll the strip into a loose snail shape and tuck into one corner of the baking dish, pushing it down gently if it's too tall. Repeat with five more sheets of pastry. By the end, you should have six snail-shaped rolls snugly fitted together, and you should have used all the jam.

5 Pour the cream mixture evenly over the pastry snails. Cover the tart with the final sheet of pastry (optional), tucking it in gently around the edges, and brush with the remaining butter. Let the tart rest for 20–30 minutes before baking.

6 Transfer the tart to the oven and bake for 15 minutes before covering with foil and baking for a further 15–20 minutes. When ready, the tart should be puffed up, fragrant, and golden brown, especially around the edge.

7 Remove the tart from the oven, drizzle over a little honey, and top with the remaining pistachios. Let cool and set for at least 20 minutes before serving. This tart is also very good served straight from the refrigerator for breakfast.

RASPBERRY AND CHOCOLATE MOUSSE

8oz (225g) semi-sweet (dark) chocolate, minimum 70% cocoa solids

1 stick (115g) unsalted butter

Pinch of fine sea salt

Scant ¼ cup (50ml) raspberry liqueur (such as Chambord)

6 eggs, separated

⅓ cup (65g) granulated sugar, plus 1 extra tbsp

⅔ cup (150ml) heavy (double) cream

⅓ cup (15g) freeze-dried raspberries, to serve (optional)

SERVES 8

This recipe was inspired by the exceptional chocolate mousse that I had at Petit Pois, a French bistro in East London. When ordered, it's brought to the table in a gigantic ceramic bowl and the portions are individually scooped out before your eyes. Although that mousse is made with orange liqueur, I've used a raspberry liqueur here and dusted it with pulverized, freeze-dried raspberries in lieu of cocoa powder. Mousse can seem a little old-fashioned, but this version feels pleasingly contemporary.

PAIR WITH A raspberry sour. Raspberry and chocolate is one of my favorite flavor combinations, and a tart, lightly sweet raspberry sour—whether a traditional Belgian framboise or a modern, raspberry-led alternative—picks up the berry elements in the mousse while tempering some of its richness.

THREE BEERS TO TRY 3 Fonteinen Hommage (Belgium); Craftwork La Framboise (New Zealand); Jester King Atrial Rubicite (US)

1 Prepare a double-boiler by filling a large saucepan with a couple of inches (5cm) of just-boiled water and placing a large, heatproof bowl or second saucepan on top. This should fit snugly inside the first saucepan, but the base should not touch the water.

2 Roughly chop the chocolate with a serrated knife and add to the bowl or saucepan above the boiling water, stirring frequently with a spatula until the chocolate melts. Add the butter and sea salt, and keep stirring until the butter has completely melted and the mixture is glossy.

3 Remove the bowl of chocolate from the stovetop. Stir frequently for several minutes until the chocolate mixture cools slightly. Slowly add the raspberry liqueur and stir rapidly to combine, to prevent the mixture splitting. Add the egg yolks and continue mixing. At this point, as the proteins bind, the mixture should begin to look granular and thicken like tar.

4 In a separate bowl, begin whisking the egg whites with a hand mixer while slowly adding ⅓ cup (65g) of sugar. Whisk the egg whites for 4–5 minutes or until you have just-firm, but not stiff, peaks. Add one-third of the egg whites to the chocolate mixture and fold in to combine. Gradually fold in the remainder of the egg whites.

5 Use the hand mixer to beat the final tablespoon of sugar into the heavy (double) cream for 2 minutes, or until the cream is thick but still just pourable. Add the sugary cream to the chocolate mix and fold in with a spatula until fully combined.

6 Pour the mousse into a large ceramic bowl or individual dishes and let chill for 4–6 hours, or until properly set before serving. If you are using freeze-dried raspberries, pulverize in a spice grinder or food processor until very finely ground. Sprinkle over the mousse, and serve.

CHAPTER 2 | LAGERS

GUIDE TO LAGER STYLES BY JEN FERGUSON

One of my favorite beery memories took place on a trip to Japan in 2011. I remember the heavens opening while Glenn and I were visiting a park, and as we ran for shelter, we stumbled across an Oktoberfest celebration—as you do in May, in a tent, in Tokyo... Within minutes we had giant masskrugs of lager in hand and were loudly bellowing the traditional German drinking song, "Ein Prosit," with our newfound friends. We spoke minimal Japanese and our friends little English, but big smiles, lots of lager, frequent repetition of drinking songs, and messy, mustard-covered hot dogs saw us through.

This is a scene we've seen replayed frequently, whether in the biergartens of Munich or at the tables right outside our stores, where one person drinking a bottle of Augustiner Lagerbier Hell soon turns into everyone drinking bottles of Augustiner Lagerbier Hell. The uniting power of lager is truly remarkable to behold—and it's about time lager received the respect it deserves.

Helping lager's cause is the fact that it's a natural with so many types of food. Around our place, pilsner paired with fish and chips is practically the law, but there are so many more options to explore.

PALE LAGER STYLES

Pale lager's fine name has been somewhat besmirched by the proliferation of weak, macro-produced beers that bear little resemblance to their professed styles (Budweiser, Foster's, and Carling, we're looking at you). But lager—proper, delicious lager—is now fighting back.

Helles and pilsner are two of the most popular pale lager styles. Originating in Germany, Helles lagers tend to be light, slightly sweet, sometimes bready, and sometimes citrusy, while pilsners are a little more crisp, bitter, and intensely refreshing.

Kölsch, another German style, is technically not a lager, as it's brewed with top-fermenting ale yeast (as opposed to bottom-fermenting lager yeast). However, it's lagered—stored in a cold environment for weeks at a time—so is often considered a hybrid style. Kölsch is beautifully biscuity, sweet, and subtle—a beer made for quaffing.

We should also throw IPL, or India Pale Lager, into the mix. Depending on which brewer you talk to, it's either an IPA brewed with lager yeast or a very hopped-up lager. Either way, it's one of our favorite styles, thanks to its bright hop aroma and light, quenching body. Every year, we wait with bated breath for this underrated style to hit the big time—alas, we're still waiting.

As a beer retailer, we get approached by a lot of breweries asking whether we'll stock their beer. Pale lager styles are a great litmus test for ascertaining a brewery's skill and quality control. There's no hiding bad brewing with a lager and you can't just throw in a bunch of hops or adjuncts to mask faults. It's got to be perfect, every time. In the quest for the perfect pale lager, it pays to look to the countries that pioneered the style.

We make no apology for the number of German lagers we recommend in this chapter: these guys have got it going on. At the end of the night, after brewers have stopped by the store for a beer (or more likely several), our crates of empties are reliably stuffed full of lagers by iconic Germany breweries such as Tegernseer, Ayinger, and Augustiner. These beers are the good stuff, and brewers know it.

The Czechs know where it's at, too. In 1842, the first Bohemian pilsner was brewed in the town of Pilsen, combining German lagering techniques with the floral, subtly spicy local Saaz hops. The town gave its name to the style and Pilsner Urquell, the "Original Pilsner," was born. Pilsner Urquell is still brewed in Pilsen, but is now owned by Asahi. However, it's so iconic we had to give it a Get Out Of Jail Free card—it's one of the only "Big Beer"-owned (at the time of writing, at least) beers we recommend in this book. Simply put, if you haven't enjoyed a Pilsner Urquell straight from the tank, you haven't lived.

Today, there are plenty of breweries specializing in great pale lager around the world, inspired by European brewers but making the styles their own. Read on to learn more about the UK's Lost and Grounded and Jack's Abby in the US.

DARK LAGER STYLES

The first time I tried Ayinger Celebrator doppelbock, I knew I'd found a beer I'd be drinking for the rest of my life. That first bottle I enjoyed just on its own, reveling in its sweet, malty richness. Then, I took home a bottle and drank it alongside some aged Gouda. The next time—some weeks later, I should add—it accompanied a big, juicy burger that Glenn grilled over coals in our backyard. It paired perfectly every time.

Most dark lagers tend to be malt-forward instead of hop-driven. Lighter styles, such as bocks, maibocks, and märzens, for example, are biscuity and bready; darker styles, such as doppelbocks, dial up sweet caramel notes and toasty aromas. A schwarzbier ("black beer") is darkest of all, yet tends to be slightly lower in alcohol (normally checking in at around 5% ABV), lighter-bodied, drier, and more bitter, with some subtle hints of coffee and chocolate.

Don't forget Baltic porters. A dark, sweet, strong porter is probably the last thing that springs to mind when you think of lagers, but a lager it is, as it's brewed with bottom-fermenting yeast. Baltic porters are all about the malt, showcasing complex flavors of nuts, caramel, toffee, and/or molasses. This makes them a natural partner for hearty, wintry food, as well as some desserts.

WHERE OLD WORLD MEETS NEW—LOST AND GROUNDED, BRISTOL, AND JACK'S ABBY, MASSACHUSETTS

A trip to Bavaria really is a trip to the lager capital of the world. Whether you're sitting in a regional brauhaus, walking through a Munich park, or devouring a pork knuckle the size of your head on the shores of Lake Tegernsee, lager is everywhere. However, in a world dominated by hops, it's unusual, outside of Germany, for modern breweries to prioritize lager—yet that's just what the UK's Lost and Grounded and Massachusetts' Jack's Abby have done.

Australians Alex Troncoso and Annie Clements set up Lost and Grounded in Bristol in 2016. Alex had cut his teeth at Australia's Little Creatures before heading up the brew team at Camden Brewery, which would become one of London's most successful craft breweries before selling to AB InBev in 2015. When Alex and Annie announced that Lost and Grounded would brew modern interpretations of classic German and Belgian beer styles, the British craft beer scene sat up and took notice.

Alex had what he describes as a lager epiphany when he drank a kellerbier on a long-ago trip to Tettnang in Germany. "What I found was a simplistic beer of complex nature—slightly hazy, lemony, piney, and crisp. From this experience, we set out to create Lost and Grounded."

Jack Hendler, founder of Jack's Abby, had a similar conversion experience. "I majored in European history and that inspired me to study brewing in the first place. When I traveled to Germany, I gained a respect for the timelessness of lagers and this traditional industry." He would go on to set up Jack's Abby in Framingham, Massachusetts, in 2011, which has quickly become a byword for iconic US craft lager (see photograph, right).

Both breweries make some of the best lagers in the world, bringing together modern innovations without sacrificing old-school tradition, techniques, and precision.

Jack says, "Our kellerbier series relies heavily on old-school brewing techniques and tradition, whereas our hoppy lagers focus on American innovation. We still use very traditional processes for even our most high-volume products, like decoction, krausening, or spunding, and cold, long fermentation."

Alex agrees. "Lager is technically challenging, and it really is a case that the whole is greater than the sum of the parts. It's the details around every step of the process and the attention required, whether it be raw material selection, milling, mashing, lautering, boiling, fermentation, maturation—every minute detail pulls together to make something wonderful."

Both remain obsessed with the possibilities that lager offers as a style. "If lager is good," says Alex, "it should be intriguing, not boring."

ESSENTIAL LOST AND GROUNDED BEERS

• Keller Pils: Ask any British beer lover which is their favorite UK lager and Keller Pils wins every time. An instant modern classic.
• Running With Spectres Special Black Beer: Alex and Annie's take on a Baltic porter. It's smooth and roasty, with big licorice and chocolate notes.

ALEX'S PERFECT PAIRING

"Anything spicy! One of our favorites to have at home is shredded beef tacos with a squeeze of lime and some hot sauce with a crisp Keller Pils."

ESSENTIAL JACK'S ABBY BEERS

• Excess IPL: Resinous, piney US hops meet lager yeast in a balanced, bitter, highly drinkable brew.
• Kiwi Rising Double IPL: A multi-award-winning big boy that incorporates more than 4lb (1.8kg) of New Zealand hops per barrel. Look out for seasonal variations of this beer too—all are excellent.

JACK'S PERFECT PAIRING:

"Salty food and liters! Don't overthink it."

FOOD PAIRINGS

Lagers lend themselves brilliantly to a wide range of food. Pale lagers are a given for chicken and seafood. They're also great with Asian foods, pizza, toasted cheese sandwiches, and so on. Dark lagers, stemming as most do from Germany, work exceptionally well with German-style foods like smoky sausages, hearty stews, and sauerkraut. They also tackle spicy foods with ease, as the malty sweetness helps tone down the heat and bring out the underlying savoriness. We love drinking a märzen or bock with a bowl of chili, a spicy burrito, or with Asian dishes such as Claire's Spicy Beef Larb (see page 79). And a rich doppelbock, like that glorious Ayinger Celebrator, is perfect for the end of a meal— with or without dessert on the side.

STYLE	CHARACTERISTICS	PAIR WITH
Kölsch	Sweet, biscuity, subtle	Salmon, shellfish, grilled pork chops
Pilsner	Crisp, bitter, citrus	Vietnamese bun cha, light seafood, Mexican cemitas
Helles	Crisp, bready, light	Clam fregola, chicken or fish with lemon sauce, hummus
IPL	Hoppy, bitter, clean	Pizza, burgers, chow mein
Maibock	Delicately sweet, toasty, peppery	Grilled asparagus, Thai larb, Korean barbecue
Märzen / Oktoberfest	Malty, toasty, crisp	Grilled sausages, ham and potatoes
Doppelbock	Strong, malty, rich	Game meats, brown butter financiers
Schwarzbier	Dark, dry, roasty	Steaks, smoked meats, Cajun blackened chicken
Dunkel	Dark, bready, caramel	Pulled pork, aged Gouda and Gruyère cheeses
Baltic porter	Dark, sweet, roasty	Hearty stews, barbecued beef, cheesecake

SAVORY PESTO TOMATO MUFFINS

3½ tbsps (50g) unsalted butter, plus extra for greasing

¾ cup (100g) pine nuts

1⅛ cups (150g) all-purpose (plain) flour

¼ cup (30g) whole-wheat (wholemeal) spelt flour (or regular whole-wheat/wholemeal flour)

1 tbsp baking powder

3 eggs

4 tbsps (60ml) olive oil

⅔ cup (150g) full-fat Greek yogurt, plus two extra tbsps

½ tsp fine sea salt

1 tsp freshly ground black pepper

2–3 tbsps pesto (err toward 2 if the pesto is quite salty)

7oz (200g) feta

24 cherry tomatoes

MAKES 12

Savory muffins might sound like an odd thing to be passionate about, but they rank among my favorite-ever dishes—not just for breakfast, but as an everyday, go-to snack. These pesto tomato muffins are my attempt at recreating the irresistible ones that celebrity chef Yotam Ottolenghi sells at his eponymous London cafés. Greek yogurt and olive oil give them a tender crumb, while the addition of nutty spelt flour makes them hearty enough to serve as a meal on their own.

PAIR WITH A light, citrusy lager. If these muffins are an ideal all-day snack, then a crisp and citrusy lager is the perfect midday-till-evening accompaniment. Choose a beer that's bright and refreshing, and which will play well with the Mediterranean flavors.

THREE BEERS TO TRY Bunker Brewing Machine Czech Pils (US); Harviestoun Schiehallion Unfiltered (UK); McLeod's Longboarder Lager (New Zealand)

1 Preheat the oven to 375°F/190°C/Gas 5 and grease a muffin pan with butter. Alternatively, use paper muffin cups if you think the pan will stick.

2 Toast the pine nuts by melting the butter in a small skillet (frying pan) and cooking them for 2–3 minutes, stirring frequently, until the butter foams up and browns and the pine nuts are toasted and smell nice and nutty. Remove from the heat and set aside.

3 Mix the flours and baking powder in a medium-sized bowl. Make a well in the center and add the eggs, olive oil, Greek yogurt, sea salt, black pepper, and pesto. Crumble the feta into the mixture in small chunks and add the toasted pine nuts. Gently fold the dry ingredients into the wet until just combined—the ingredients need to be fully incorporated, but be careful not to overmix.

4 Spoon the batter into the muffin pan until each mold is half-full. Delicately place one cherry tomato in each mold, but don't press down, as you don't want the tomato to sink to the bottom. Then, spoon over the remaining batter until all the tomatoes are covered and each mold is filled to the top. Stick another cherry tomato on top and press down gently so it's just wedged in the batter (though it will mostly be exposed).

5 Bake the muffins for 15–18 minutes, rotating the muffin pan after 10 minutes if your oven has hot spots. The muffins are done when risen and deep golden on top. Remove from the oven and let cool in the pan for 5 minutes before transferring to a cooling rack. (If you'd like to eat a muffin warm, wait until the tomato in the middle is no longer molten.) Once the muffins have cooled completely, they can be stored in an airtight container in the refrigerator for 3–4 days.

SALMON RICE BOWLS WITH SOY-CURED EGG YOLKS

Heaping 1 cup (250g) sushi rice

1⅓ cups (330ml) cold water

2½ tbsps rice vinegar

2 tbsps granulated sugar

1 tsp fine sea salt

7oz (200g) sushi-grade salmon fillet, skin removed

3½ oz (100g) salmon roe

Nori, sliced into thin strips, to garnish

FOR THE SOY-CURED EGG YOLKS

3 tbsps soy sauce

1½ tbsps sake

1 tsp granulated sugar

2 eggs

SERVES 2

In Japanese restaurants, *donburi* (rice bowls) are one of my favorite things to order. You can choose from a number of toppings, from sea bass to sea urchin. In this iteration, I go for the classic salmon *sashimi* and *ikura* (salmon roe) combination. For added decadence, I've also riffed by adding a soy sauce-cured egg yolk to the mix. Think of these rice bowls as a home cook's simpler, deconstructed take on sushi— no rolling required.

PAIR WITH A kölsch. Technically made with top-fermenting ale yeast, but stored at cold temperatures for long periods of time the way a lager would be, this hybrid style hails originally from Cologne, Germany, and is known for its easy-drinking characteristics and crisp finish.

THREE BEERS TO TRY Früh Kölsch (Germany); Mühlen Kölsch (Germany); Sierra Nevada Kölsch (US)

1 Prepare the soy-cured egg yolks about 6 hours before you plan to eat. Add the soy sauce, sake, and sugar to a ramekin or small bowl, and stir until the sugar dissolves. Over a separate bowl, carefully break open the first egg and let the white drain into the bowl—you can use the egg shells to separate the yolk from the white, but I prefer to use my hands to minimize the chance that the yolk will break. Once the egg is fully separated, gently place the yolk in the soy sauce mixture. Repeat for the second egg. Cover the ramekin or bowl with plastic wrap (clingfilm) and chill in the fridge for 6 hours.

2 Rinse the sushi rice with cold water through a fine-meshed sieve for 3–4 minutes, stirring gently with your hands, or until the water runs clear. Shake out any excess water. Put the rice in a medium-sized saucepan, add the water, and cook over medium-high heat. As soon as the water begins to boil, cover the pan and reduce the heat to low. Let simmer for 10 minutes, then remove from the heat and let the rice rest for 30 minutes, or until the remainder of the water has been absorbed. Do not remove the lid at any point.

3 Add the rice vinegar, sugar, and sea salt to a small bowl, and stir well until the sugar and salt begin dissolving. Pour over the rice and gently fold to combine with a spatula. Divide the rice between two bowls and let cool to room temperature.

4 Prepare the sashimi. Using a very sharp knife, carefully cut the salmon into ¼-inch (5mm) pieces, slicing on a bias. Arrange the slices over one half of each rice bowl.

5 Spoon the salmon roe to one side of the salmon in each bowl. Gently remove the egg yolks from the soy-sauce mixture and place one in the center of each bowl. If you wish, drizzle some of the leftover soy-sauce mixture over the salmon. Garnish each bowl with the sliced nori.

VIETNAMESE PORK BELLY WITH NOODLES, FRIZZLED SHALLOTS, AND WATERMELON SALAD

1lb (450g) pork belly, cut into 2-inch (5cm) cubes

1½ tbsps vegetable oil

4 tbsps light brown sugar

2-inch (5cm) piece of fresh ginger, peeled and finely chopped

2 garlic cloves, finely chopped

2 tbsps fish sauce

2 tbsps soy sauce

2 cups (500ml) water

2–3 bird's-eye chili peppers, finely chopped

Juice of 1 lime

Small bunch of cilantro (fresh coriander)

Handful of roasted peanuts, roughly chopped

FOR THE FRIZZLED SHALLOTS

3 echalion (banana) shallots, thinly sliced

1 tbsp all-purpose (plain) flour

½ tsp fine sea salt

1¼ cups (300ml) vegetable oil

Freshly ground black pepper

(Ingredients continue overleaf)

Now *here* is a meal that I want to eat whenever the weather is hot, in the sun; its vague tropicality makes even an average day feel like a vacation. Unctuous pieces of pork belly are simmered in a Vietnamese caramel sauce until nearly melting. They're then served on top of coconut-scented rice noodles, dressed with frizzled shallots, and complemented by a refreshing watermelon salad. Sweet, savory, spicy, sour; tender, crispy, crunchy, toothsome: this powerhouse dish really does it all.

PAIR WITH A Bavarian pilsner. A classic, crisp, and quenching pilsner is the ideal accompaniment here—it refreshes without competing with the bold flavors at play, and is equally suited to summery weather.

THREE BEERS TO TRY Badische Staatsbrauerei Rothaus Pils Tannenzäpfle (Germany); Lost and Grounded Keller Pils (UK); Victory Prima Pils (US)

1 Bring a large pot of water to a boil on the stovetop, add the pork belly, and blanch for 2–3 minutes. Use a slotted spoon or spider strainer to transfer the pork to a paper towel-lined plate and pat to dry.

2 Add the vegetable oil and brown sugar to a wok or large skillet (frying pan). Cook over high heat until the sugar melts and starts to caramelize. Add the pork and cook, tossing to coat in the sugar mixture, for 2–3 minutes, or until it begins to brown. Add the ginger and garlic, and cook for a further 30 seconds. Next, add the fish sauce, soy sauce, and water—the pork pieces should be just covered. Bring to a boil, then reduce to a simmer. Cover and cook for approximately 1–1¼ hours, or until the pork is fork-tender.

3 Meanwhile, make the frizzled shallots. Add the shallots to a bowl, along with the flour, sea salt, and a good amount of freshly ground black pepper, and toss lightly to coat. Heat the vegetable oil in another large skillet over high heat until it is hot, but not smoking. Add one shallot to test the heat; the oil is hot enough when the shallot starts sizzling rapidly. Add half the shallots and cook for 5–7 minutes, using kitchen tongs to flip them over so that they cook evenly. When the shallots are golden brown, use a slotted spoon or spider strainer to transfer them to a paper towel-lined plate. Repeat for the second batch of shallots.

(Method continues overleaf)

1 tbsp clear honey

2 tbsps rice vinegar

2 tbsps sesame oil

Juice of ½ lime

2 tsps soy sauce

14oz (400g) seedless
   peeled watermelon, cut
   into ½-inch (1cm) pieces

2oz (60g) watercress or
   spinach

FOR THE COCONUT
RICE NOODLES

8oz (225g) rice noodles

1 tsp fine sea salt

2 tbsps coconut oil, melted

SERVES 4

4 Shortly before the pork is ready, prepare the watermelon salad. To make the dressing, whisk together the honey, rice vinegar, sesame oil, lime juice, and soy sauce in a small bowl. Add the watermelon to a large bowl and pour over the dressing. Set aside and leave the flavors to blend for 10 minutes.

5 Once the pork is tender, remove the lid from the wok or skillet and raise the heat to high. Toss the pork until the excess moisture evaporates. Add the chili peppers and lime juice once the liquid has nearly reduced (carefully, as the hot sugar may spit) and continue cooking until it reduces to a sticky glaze. Remove from the heat and let cool slightly.

6 For the coconut rice noodles, add the noodles to a saucepan and pour over just enough boiling water to cover. Stir through the sea salt. Cover and let stand for 3 minutes, or until the noodles are tender. Drain and rinse the noodles quickly with cold water to stop them cooking further. Toss the coconut oil through the noodles to prevent them sticking.

7 Add the watercress or spinach to the watermelon salad and toss to combine.

8 Divide the noodles between four plates and top with the pork pieces, plus any extra dribbles of glaze. Garnish with the frizzled shallots, cilantro (fresh coriander), and chopped peanuts. Serve immediately with the watermelon salad.

HUMMUS WITH CHERMOULA

1¼ cups (250g) dried chickpeas

1½ tsps baking soda (bicarbonate of soda), divided

2 garlic cloves, smashed

Juice of 2 lemons

¾ cup (175ml) tahini (buy the best-quality tahini you can find; I love Al Yaman)

1½ tsps fine sea salt

½ cup (125ml) ice-cold water

Pinch of za'atar

Warm pitas, to serve

FOR THE CHERMOULA

Small bunch of cilantro (fresh coriander)

Small bunch of fresh parsley

Small bunch of fresh mint

2 garlic cloves, peeled

3 tbsps lemon juice

4 tbsps extra virgin olive oil, plus extra for drizzling

2 tsps ground cumin

2 tsps paprika

¾ tsp cayenne pepper

¾ tsp fine sea salt

SERVES 4

I never had strong opinions about hummus until I tried the recipe from Yotam Ottolenghi's seminal cookbook, *Jerusalem*. His Israeli-style hummus distinguishes itself from grainy, grocery-store counterparts with an unbelievably silken, whipped consistency, as well as a generous ratio of tahini. This hummus borrows from that tradition: it's airy, velveteen, and absolutely delicious. So delicious, in fact, it makes up for the fact that you need to start prepping it the night before. Choices for topping border on the infinite, but I complement my hummus with chermoula and za'atar.

PAIR WITH A classic helles. If hummus works as well for lunch and snacks as it does for dinner, then, hell, helles is just the same. Effervescent, refreshing, and lightly sweet, helles—like hummus—is an excellent all-rounder.

THREE BEERS TO TRY Augustiner Lagerbier Hell (Germany); Hill Farmstead Marie (US); Thornbridge Lukas (UK)

1 Prepare the chickpeas the night before cooking. Add the dried chickpeas to a large bowl with ¾ teaspoon of the baking soda (bicarbonate of soda) and cover with double the amount of water. Let soak overnight, or for at least 8–12 hours.

2 The next day, drain and rinse the chickpeas. Add to a medium saucepan with the garlic and remaining ¾ teaspoon of baking soda. Cover with 2–3 inches (5–7.5cm) of cold water and bring to a boil. Reduce to a simmer and let cook for at least 45 minutes to 1 hour, or until the chickpeas are falling apart, occasionally skimming off any foam or chickpea skins that float to the surface. Start tasting the chickpeas after 30 minutes; different varieties cook more quickly than others. 10 minutes before the chickpeas are cooked, strain and reserve about ½ cup (100g) to use as a topping later.

3 While the chickpeas are cooking, prepare the chermoula. Add all the ingredients to a food processor and blend well for 2–3 minutes, or until the mixture forms a thick paste. Transfer the paste to a small bowl and set aside. Wash and dry the food processor, as you'll need it to make the hummus.

4 Once the chickpeas are extremely tender and falling apart, drain and transfer to the food processor while still warm. Turn the food processor to high and blend the chickpeas to a paste. While the motor is still running, add the lemon juice, tahini, and sea salt, pausing to scrape down the sides of the bowl with a spatula to ensure everything is fully mixed. Then add the ice-cold water in a steady stream. Continue blending for 5 minutes, or until the hummus is extremely smooth and airy.

5 Transfer the hummus to a large serving dish, using the back of a spoon to create a large depression in the middle. Drizzle over the chermoula—you may have some left over, depending on how much you wish to add—as well as an additional tablespoon or two of extra virgin olive oil. Finish off with the chickpeas you reserved earlier and a sprinkling of za'atar. Serve with a pile of warm pita breads on the side.

CHICKPEA-FLOUR CRÊPES WITH SAUTÉED KALE

3½ tbsps olive oil, divided, plus extra for frying

1 tbsp (15g) butter

1 large onion, thinly sliced

¾ tsp fine sea salt, plus extra for seasoning

3¼ cups (300g) chickpea (gram) flour

1⅔ cups (400ml) cold water

1 tsp cumin seeds

⅜ cup (55g) Marcona almonds

3oz (85g) Manchego cheese, shaved

Zest of 1 lemon

Freshly ground black pepper

4 fried eggs, to serve (optional)

FOR THE SAUTÉED KALE

7oz (200g) curly kale, stems and ribs removed

2½ tbsps olive oil

2 garlic cloves, thinly sliced

6 tbsps (90ml) vegetable stock

¾ tsp smoked paprika

2 tbsps sherry vinegar

Fine sea salt and freshly ground black pepper

SERVES 4

Called *socca* in the South of France and *farinata* in Italy, chickpea-flour crêpes are some of the simplest pancakes that it's possible to make. With their hearty, earthy flavor, they work especially well with savory toppings. In this recipe, they take on something of an Iberian guise, courtesy of Manchego, toasted Marcona almonds, and kale perfumed with smoked paprika. To make them extra-hearty, a fried egg wouldn't go amiss.

PAIR WITH A biscuity lager. Pick a beer with a malt-driven flavor profile that picks up the earthiness of the crêpes and the warm, toasty notes of the Marcona almonds.

THREE BEERS TO TRY Ayinger Jahrhundert Bier (Germany); Braybrooke Beer Co Keller Lager (UK); Suarez Family While (US)

1 First, caramelize the onions for the crêpes. Heat 1 tablespoon of the olive oil and the butter in a large, nonstick skillet (frying pan) over medium heat until the butter is just melting. Add the onion, reduce the heat to medium-low, and season with a large pinch of sea salt. Stir frequently, ensuring the heat is low enough so the onion doesn't darken too quickly, and cook for 30–40 minutes, or until caramelized—the onion should be sticky, soft, and dark. Transfer to a small bowl and set the skillet aside.

2 To prepare the crêpe batter, add the chickpea (gram) flour, cold water, 2 tablespoons of the olive oil, the cumin seeds, ¾ teaspoon of sea salt, and a few good grinds of black pepper to a large bowl. Whisk well until the batter is completely smooth. Let rest.

3 Meanwhile, prepare the kale by rinsing thoroughly, patting dry, and chopping roughly. Heat the olive oil in the skillet over medium heat. Add the garlic and cook for several minutes, or until it is starting to turn golden. Add the kale in batches—it may sizzle and splatter at first—and stir for 1–2 minutes, or until it is evenly coated with oil and has wilted enough to fit in the skillet. Pour in the vegetable stock, sprinkle in the smoked paprika, and stir everything briefly to combine. Keep the heat on medium, cover the skillet, and cook for 5 minutes.

4 Meanwhile, toast the almonds in a small skillet (frying pan) over medium-high heat, tossing frequently, for 4–5 minutes, or until the almonds have darkened in color and smell toasty. Transfer to a small bowl and let cool.

5 Once the kale is cooked, pour in the sherry vinegar. Turn the heat up to high and toss until most of the excess moisture has evaporated. Season with a pinch of sea salt and black pepper, then transfer to a bowl. Clean and dry the skillet.

6 Finally, make the crêpes by whisking the caramelized onions through the batter. Heat the remaining ½ tablespoon of olive oil in the skillet over medium-high heat. Ladle a quarter of the batter into the skillet—it should make a 7–8-inch (18–20cm) circle—and cook the crêpe for 2 minutes, or until the edge solidifies and small bubbles appear across the surface. Loosen the edge with a spatula, carefully flip, and cook the crêpe on the other side for a further 1½–2 minutes. Transfer to a plate and cover; alternatively, keep the crêpe warm on a baking sheet in the oven at its lowest setting.

7 Repeat for the other three crêpes, monitoring the skillet's heat so that they cook evenly without burning. Use extra olive oil between batches if the crêpes start to stick.

8 To serve, place a crêpe on each plate and top with the kale. Roughly chop the toasted almonds and sprinkle over the crêpes, then top with the shaved Manchego and lemon zest. Add a fried egg to each crêpe, if you wish.

THREE-CHEESE TOASTED SANDWICHES WITH TOMATO BISQUE

About 4 tbsps (60g) unsalted butter

8 thick slices of challah

4 slices American cheese

8 *bocconcini* (mini mozzarella balls)

2oz (55g) herbed goat's cheese

FOR THE TOMATO BISQUE

1 tbsp (15g) unsalted butter

1 large white onion, finely diced

2 garlic cloves, chopped

2 tbsps tomato paste (purée)

1 28oz (800g) can crushed (chopped) tomatoes in juice

4 cups (1 liter) chicken or vegetable stock (or water)

1 tsp red wine vinegar

2–3 tbsps light brown sugar

½ cup (125ml) heavy (double) cream, plus extra for drizzling

2½ tbsps olive oil

2 tsps cumin seeds

Fine sea salt and freshly ground black pepper

Small bunch of fresh basil leaves, to garnish

SERVES 4

If you ask me, childhood comfort food is sacred—and few dishes are more soothing than a toasted cheese sandwich paired with a bowl of tomato soup. It can be tempting to gussy up old favorites with sophisticated, adult ingredients, but you can also risk losing their original essence (and pleasure) by overcomplicating things. In this recipe, I strike a balance between high and low: these toasted cheese sandwiches are made with bright orange American cheese, but also with *bocconcini* (mini mozzarella balls) and herbed goat's cheese. By toasting all four sides of the bread—a technique learned from food website Serious Eats—you get impeccable crunch and melt. As for the soup: it's a classic tomato bisque, but the last-minute addition of toasted cumin seeds adds a pleasant aroma and textural contrast.

PAIR WITH A classic helles lager. Like a perfect toasted cheese sandwich, a well-made helles—bright, bready, and slightly sweet—is an unimprovable entity. Its satisfying simplicity makes it an ideal pairing partner.

THREE BEERS TO TRY Cloudwater Helles (UK); North End Brewery Pacific Blonde—Kapiti Lager (New Zealand); Tegernseer Hell (Germany)

1 To prepare the tomato bisque, melt the butter in a large saucepan over medium heat. Add the onion and season lightly with sea salt and black pepper. Cook, stirring frequently, for approximately 10 minutes, or until the onion is very soft. Add the garlic and cook for a further 2 minutes, or until it starts turning golden. Add the tomato paste (purée), stir to combine, and cook for another 1–2 minutes.

2 Add the crushed (chopped) tomatoes and juice to the saucepan, and stir before adding the stock or water. Increase the heat to high and bring the mixture to a boil before reducing to a simmer. Add the red wine vinegar and 2 tablespoons of the sugar. Cook for 1–1¼ hours, or until the bisque reduces by nearly half, is very thick, and the flavors have deepened. Stir often and taste throughout the cooking process, adjusting the seasoning accordingly. Because the bisque will reduce a good deal, be sure not to salt too heavily at the start.

3 Just before the bisque is ready, taste for sweetness and add the remaining tablespoon of brown sugar if necessary, plus any additional salt to taste. Remove from the heat and let cool for 5 minutes. Use an immersion blender to blend the bisque carefully until it is completely smooth. (Although you can do this in a regular blender, you may have to work in batches and let the bisque cool for longer beforehand.) Return the bisque to the stovetop on the lowest heat. Slowly drizzle in the heavy (double) cream, stirring to combine, then leave the bisque on the stovetop to keep warm while you make the cheese sandwiches.

(Method continues overleaf)

4 To make the sandwiches, melt 1 tablespoon of the butter in a large skillet (frying pan)—preferably one made from cast iron—over medium heat. Place four slices of challah in the skillet and toast for 5 minutes, rotating occasionally so they toast evenly, until they are lightly golden on the underside. Transfer the slices to a plate, toasted sides up: you'll be using these to make the first two sandwiches. On two of the pieces, place 1 slice of American cheese (torn into smaller pieces if necessary, to prevent any overhang), plus 2 *bocconcini* (mini mozzarella balls) sliced in half and a few small blobs of goat's cheese. Seal the sandwiches with the other two slices of bread, with the toasted sides on the inside (this will ensure the cheese melts evenly).

5 Melt another tablespoon of butter in the skillet. Return the sandwiches to the skillet and cook over medium heat for 3–4 minutes on each side, rotating frequently and pressing down lightly with a spatula until both sides are crisp and golden brown, and the cheese is gooey. Transfer to a plate and tent with foil. Repeat the process for the other two cheese sandwiches, adding more butter if necessary.

6 Before serving, finish the bisque by heating the olive oil in a small skillet (frying pan) over medium-high heat. Add the cumin seeds and stir frequently for about 2 minutes, or until the seeds are fragrant and darkened. Remove from the heat.

7 To serve, ladle the tomato bisque into four bowls and top with a drizzle of the toasted cumin seeds and their oil, plus an extra drizzle of heavy cream. Garnish with a few torn basil leaves. Slice each sandwich in half and serve alongside the bisque.

BEER AND CHEESE

BY CLAIRE BULLEN

It is a truth all too rarely acknowledged that cheese pairs better with beer than with wine. The credit for this goes to beer's versatility and also its enormous range of flavors: caramelized malts evoke aged Goudas and Alpine cheeses; mixed-fermentation beers share aromatics (and sometimes microbes) with pungent, washed-rind varieties; lactose-infused beers match cheese's creamy mouthfeel; herbaceous saisons recall milder sheep and goat's cheeses; and on and on. Wine's fruit flavors and bright acidity primarily contrast with cheese's salt and fat, whereas beer presents numerous avenues for both contrasting and complementary pairings (see page 22). Beer's carbonation helps temper the richness of cheese, too.

As Garrett Oliver opined during an interview at Murray's Cheese in New York, beer and cheese even share the same roots. Both begin with grass—grass as feed or grass as grains—which is transformed via processing and fermentation into something greater. Today, the two also share much the same ethos. Following mass industrialization and homogenization during the 20th century, beer and cheese have both experienced recent, artisan-led revivals bent on independence. Cheesemakers are discovering historic recipes made according to generations-old techniques, while brewers are also looking to bygone traditions to re-establish heritage.

If you'd like to host a beer and cheese pairing night of your own, but are unsure of where to start, don't fret about memorizing elaborate rules. Happily, the two get along so well that it's difficult to go wrong.

WHICH BEERS AND CHEESES TO BUY

For starters, it helps if you're beginning with high-quality products. Skip the shrink-wrapped, mass-market cheese and go to a local cheese store, farmers' market, or grocery store with an artisanal cheese counter. Select cheeses whose lineage can be traced to independent makers. The same metric applies to your beer, of course.

London cheesemonger Ned Palmer, host of pairing events at Hop Burns & Black, also recommends having a wide array of options on the table. To create a diverse cheese board, opt for a traditional Cheddar, an Alpine cheese like Comté, a bloomy-rind cheese like Camembert, a goat's cheese, a blue cheese, and a washed-rind cheese. The same applies to beer: pick an IPA, a porter or stout, a malt-driven Belgian or German style, a lager, and a sour.

TIPS FOR PAIRING BEER AND CHEESE

Ned goes on to say, "Try them together in a spirit of open-minded exploration, rather than trying to make definitive one-to-one matches." Broadly, he counsels, matching cheeses and beers of similar intensities is a good place to start: think a delicate goat's cheese with a wheat beer, or a boozy tripel with a washed-rind cheese.

Then, begin to investigate both complementary and contrasting pairing options. You may find that one beer draws out a cheese's lactic sweetness, while another makes it taste pithy and citrusy, so it's worth sampling many different combinations to discover which you enjoy.

Texture, too, is important to keep in mind. As Ned says: "I like to think about mouthfeel, which I also think can be complementary or contrasting. Rich, velvety beers are nice with very creamy cheeses, the whole forming a luxurious emulsion. Or, I might match a very creamy, unctuous cheese, like a ripe Camembert, with a lager; the sharper carbonation makes a nice foil to the mouth-coating texture of the cheese."

No matter what you do, you can't go wrong with a perfect pairing: porter and Stilton is a bulletproof match.

CLAM FREGOLA WITH SAFFRON

2¼ lb (1kg) small clams

Large pinch of saffron strands

2 tbsps boiling water

3 tbsps olive oil

3 echalion (banana) shallots, finely diced

2 garlic cloves, chopped

1 tsp red pepper (dried chili) flakes

2 tbsps tomato paste (purée)

1½ cups (350ml) white vermouth

4 cups (1 liter) chicken stock

2⅓ cups (400g) fregola (or use pearl/Israeli/giant couscous)

Zest of 1 lemon

Small bunch of fresh parsley, roughly chopped

Fine sea salt

SERVES 4

Sardinian in origin, *fregola* are bead-sized spheres of pasta that have a knack for soaking up sauces. In this case, a heady, vermouth-based sauce, which also features brilliant-red tomato paste (purée), a good sprinkle of red pepper (dried chili) flakes, vibrant strands of saffron, and a heap of briny clams. Rich and stew-like, this dish offers a very Mediterranean take on comfort eating.

PAIR WITH A classic German helles lager. Less piquantly bitter than pilsners, helles lagers offer a subtle, honeyed sweetness alongside a crisp, effervescent body. As a style, they pair well with seafood. Here, I like how the beer's delicate sweetness plays with the perfumed vermouth notes.

THREE BEERS TO TRY Mahr's Bräu Helles (Germany); New Glarus Brewing Two Women (US); Weihenstephaner Original (Germany)

1 Clean the clams about 1 hour before cooking, discarding any that are open or broken. Fill a large bowl with cold water and add the clams. Let sit for 20 minutes. Transfer the clams to a second bowl filled with cold, salted water and let sit for a further 20 minutes. Finally, transfer the clams to a third bowl of cold water. Using a scrubbing brush, remove any grit left on the clams. Rinse the clams and set aside.

2 Add the saffron to a ramekin or small bowl, pour over the boiling water, and set aside.

3 Heat the olive oil in a large saucepan over medium heat and add the shallots. Cook the shallots for about 3 minutes, stirring frequently, or until softened. Add the garlic and cook for a further minute before stirring through the red pepper (dried chili) flakes. Cook for 30 seconds, then add the tomato paste (purée). Stir through and cook for 2 minutes more, or until the shallots have darkened.

4 Pour the vermouth into the saucepan, increase the heat to high to bring the mixture to a boil, and then reduce to a simmer. Add half the clams to the pan. Cover and cook for approximately 5 minutes, or until the clams are just opened. Transfer the open clams to a bowl with a slotted spoon or spider strainer and discard any that remain closed. Repeat for the remaining clams.

5 Once the clams have been removed, you will be left with a fragrant broth. Add the chicken stock to this broth and bring to a rolling boil over high heat. Add the fregola or pearl couscous, and cook according to packet instructions, or until al dente—this will take about 10–12 minutes. Add an extra splash of water during cooking if the mixture reduces too much; it should be thick and stew-like, with little remaining liquid.

6 Remove the fregola or pearl couscous from the heat and stir through the clams and saffron mixture. (The broth will be hot enough to reheat the clams.) Season to taste with sea salt, if necessary (you may not need any, as the clams are already quite saline).

7 To serve, divide the clams between four bowls and top with the lemon zest and chopped parsley. Serve immediately.

CURRIED LAMB DUMPLINGS

1 onion, roughly chopped

3 garlic cloves, smashed

Thumb-sized piece of fresh ginger, peeled and roughly chopped

1lb (450g) ground (minced) lamb

5 scallions (spring onions), thinly sliced and green parts only

Small bunch of cilantro (fresh coriander), finely chopped

½ tsp fine sea salt

2 tbsps tomato paste (purée)

1 tbsp curry powder

½ tsp hot chili powder

½ tsp ground cinnamon

½ tsp ground cloves

½ tsp ground turmeric

4 tsps sesame oil

1 egg

60–70 dumpling wrappers, defrosted if frozen

Freshly ground black pepper

Soy sauce and sriracha (optional), to serve

MAKES 60 TO 70 DUMPLINGS

Making dumplings at home might seem difficult if you've never done it before—and, as with pancakes, the first couple may not come out quite right. But keep going: once you've got the rhythm down, half of the fun is in the meditative, repetitive action of folding, pleating, and crimping. You could make your own dough from scratch, but frozen dumpling wrappers work just as well, so this certainly isn't necessary. Made from curried lamb, and vaguely inspired by hearty Nepalese momos, these rich and spicy dumplings are perfect for a chilly night.

PAIR WITH A kölsch-style lager. I like the way the style's subtle fruitiness and dry finish juxtapose with the richness and fattiness of the spiced lamb filling; a frothy pint offers just the right kind of contrast and refreshment.

THREE BEERS TO TRY Brasserie Dieu de Ciel! Sentinelle (Canada); Mike Hess Brewing Claritas (US); Orbit Nico (UK)

1 Add the onion, garlic, and ginger to a food processor, and pulse until very finely chopped—almost liquefied. Transfer the mixture to a large bowl, along with the lamb.

2 Add the scallions (spring onions), cilantro (fresh coriander), sea salt, tomato paste (purée), spices, sesame oil, and egg to the lamb mixture. Using a spoon (or preferably your hands), mix the ingredients until well blended. Check for seasoning by microwaving a pinch of the lamb mixture for roughly 20 seconds and sampling, then season to taste, if needed.

3 To make the dumplings, ensure you have a small bowl of cold water at hand. Take a dumpling wrapper and use a finger to dab water around the circumference (this will help it stick together). Place a teaspoon- to a teaspoon-and-a-half-sized ball of lamb mixture in the center of the wrapper and shape so that it's slightly oblong. Gently fold the wrapper in half, pressing out any air inside, and lightly seal the edge. Make small pleats along the edge with your thumb and forefinger. Once the dumpling is shaped and sealed, transfer to a cutting board and cover lightly with a dish towel to stop it drying out. Continue making dumplings until the lamb mixture is used up.

4 To cook the dumplings, line a bamboo steamer with parchment (baking) paper and place snugly over a pot of simmering water (making sure the water doesn't touch the base of the steamer). Place a batch of dumplings inside—check they aren't touching, so they don't stick together—cover, and steam for 8–10 minutes, or until cooked through. Repeat with the remaining dumplings, cooking them in batches.

5 Serve the dumplings with soy sauce and also sriracha, if you want more heat.

Tip: Uncooked dumplings freeze well. To freeze, line a container with parchment (baking) paper, dust with flour, and gently place the dumplings inside. You can also steam dumplings from frozen; just increase the cooking time to 18–20 minutes.

SLOW-FERMENTED 'NDUJA PIZZA

FOR THE DOUGH

Scant 3 cups (350g) all-purpose (plain) flour, plus extra for dusting

1¼ tsps fine sea salt

¼ tsp active-dry yeast

7fl oz (210ml) room-temperature water

FOR THE TOMATO SAUCE

1 28oz (800g) can whole peeled plum tomatoes

2 tsps granulated sugar

1 tsp flaky sea salt (such as Maldon)

3 tbsps extra virgin olive oil

TO MAKE THE PIZZAS

Vegetable oil, for greasing

3½ oz (100g) *bocconcini* (mini mozzarella balls), halved

Parmigiano Reggiano, shaved

1–2 tbsps extra virgin olive oil

8oz (225g) 'nduja

Small bunch of fresh basil leaves and 2 large handfuls of arugula (rocket), to garnish

MAKES TWO 12-INCH (30CM) PIZZAS

You really can make restaurant-quality pizza at home. Begin with slow-fermented dough—this recipe is a slight tweak on Jim Lahey's classic, no-knead pizza dough recipe—that rises over the course of 18 hours. Top it with a simple, no-cook tomato sauce, inspired by the Smitten Kitchen blog (I'm a Chicagoan by birth, so I favor a generous amount of this), and some of the best-quality ingredients you can find: in this case, 'nduja (a spicy, spreadable Calabrian sausage), arugula (rocket) leaves, and two types of cheese. Sure, it takes some pre-planning and involves more work than calling for a pizza delivery, but it's worth the effort.

PAIR WITH A hop-driven IPL. A number of breweries have started brewing lagers with the same bold, fruit-driven hop profiles that characterize their IPAs. An IPL is the perfect pizza beer: its light body is refreshing, while the hop profile stands up to more potent ingredients (like the 'nduja, in this case).

THREE BEERS TO TRY Buxton Brewery Dorway IPL (UK); Jack's Abby Excess IPL (US); Liberty Brewing Halo Pilsner (New Zealand)

1 The dough needs 18 hours to ferment, so begin the day before. Mix the flour, sea salt, and yeast in a medium-sized bowl. Slowly pour in the water, stirring to combine with a wooden spoon, until the dough comes together (you may find it easier to work the dough with your hands). If the dough is very sticky, add a little extra flour. Transfer the dough to a large bowl, seal tightly with plastic wrap (clingfilm), and let rise undisturbed in a warm place for 18 hours.

2 When the dough is ready, preheat the oven to its hottest setting and coat a large baking sheet with a thin film of oil.

3 Meanwhile, prepare the tomato sauce. Pour the tomatoes into a sieve over a bowl and let sit for 20 minutes, or until most of the watery liquid has run out, gently pressing the tomatoes with a spatula to help them drain. Save or discard the tomato juice, and transfer the drained tomatoes to a separate bowl. Add the sugar, sea salt, and olive oil, and blend with an immersion blender (or in a food processor) until the sauce is smooth. Set aside.

4 To make the pizzas, generously dust the countertop with flour and use a spatula to scrape the dough out of the bowl—the consistency changes during fermentation and it will now be very sticky, stretchy, and soft. Use a dough scraper or sharp knife to divide the dough into two equal portions. Set one aside and cover with a damp cloth to stop it drying out.

(Method continues overleaf)

5 Take one of the halves of dough, then dust your hands and the top of the dough with more flour. Shape the dough into a small mound and start pulling from the outer edges, rotating as you go, until you have a large, thin circle. You can do this while holding the dough in mid-air or on the countertop—whichever is easier. Continue pulling and stretching the dough until it is about 12 inches (30cm) across (don't worry if it is more oblong than circular).

6 Carefully transfer the pizza base to the oiled baking sheet. Dollop half the tomato sauce in the middle and spread evenly across the pizza with the back of a spoon, leaving a small margin around the edge. Top the pizza with the halved *bocconcini* (mini mozzarella balls) and a scattering of shaved Parmigiano Reggiano. Drizzle over the extra virgin olive oil.

7 Bake the pizza in the oven for 8–10 minutes—the crust should be puffy around the edge and darkening, and the tomato sauce sizzling. Remove the pizza from the oven, top with half the 'nduja (using your hands to dollop it evenly over the surface), and return to the oven for a further 2 minutes. (Adding the 'nduja at this late stage stops it charring.) Remove the pizza from the oven and let cool for 5 minutes. Meanwhile, prepare the second pizza and bake as before.

8 Before serving, garnish each pizza with torn basil leaves and a generous handful of arugula (rocket).

Tip: If you are only making one pizza, the remaining dough can be transferred to a small bowl, covered tightly with plastic wrap (clingfilm), and kept in the refrigerator for several days.

COD EN PAPILLOTE WITH HERB SALSA AND LAVENDER NEW POTATOES

Olive oil, for frying

2 tbsps brined capers, rinsed and patted dry

1 lemon

1 echalion (banana) shallot, very thinly sliced

2 large cod fillets or other white fish (about 9oz/250g each)

7oz (200g) cherry tomatoes, halved

Fine sea salt and freshly ground black pepper

Cooking fish fillets in a parchment (baking) paper bag may not sound particularly glamorous—certainly not as glamorous as *en papillote* might suggest—but this preparation technique is a winner for speed and simplicity. Within its sealed environment, the fish steams gently while being perfumed with whatever aromatics you've added. Make a feature of this and invite your guests to slice open their bags at the table; the billowing waft of fragrant steam that emerges is the best kind of culinary spectacle.

PAIR WITH A Czech pilsner. With their delicate sweetness, ever-so-subtle touch of buttery diacetyl, and snappy bitterness, Czech pilsners are a food-friendly style. They should match this dish's fresh, Mediterranean flavors well.

THREE BEERS TO TRY Bohem Brewery Amos Czech Pilsner (UK); Kout na Šumavě Brewery Koutský 12° Světlý Ležák (Czech Republic); Pilsner Urquell (Czech Republic)

FOR THE HERB SALSA

4 tbsps extra virgin olive oil

Small handful of fresh flat-leaf parsley

2 tsps fresh tarragon leaves

1 green chili pepper, roughly chopped

1 garlic clove, roughly chopped

Pinch of fine sea salt

FOR THE LAVENDER NEW POTATOES

1lb (450g) baby new potatoes or fingerling potatoes, washed and scrubbed (with any larger potatoes halved)

2 tbsps (30g) unsalted butter

1 tsp dried culinary lavender

Fine sea salt

SERVES 2

1 Preheat the oven to 400°F/200°C/Gas 6.

2 To make the herb salsa, add all the ingredients to a food processor and blend until the herbs are coarsely chopped. Set aside.

3 To make the fried capers to garnish the cod, fill a small skillet (frying pan) with just enough olive oil to cover the capers completely and heat on high. After several minutes, test the oil is hot enough by adding one caper; if it sizzles rapidly, add the rest carefully, as they may spit. Fry for 2–3 minutes, or until the capers are crisp and have opened slightly. Remove the skillet from the heat and use a slotted spoon or spider strainer to transfer the capers to a paper towel-lined plate. Set aside.

4 For the lavender potatoes, place the potatoes in a medium-sized saucepan, just cover with water, and turn the heat to medium-high. Cover the pan until the water reaches a boil. Salt the water generously, reduce to a simmer, and cover the pan again. Cook the potatoes for approximately 12–15 minutes, or until fork-tender.

5 Meanwhile, prepare the cod. For each fish fillet, you'll need a large sheet of parchment (baking) paper, at least four or five times the size of the fillet. Fold the paper in half and then unfold it, so you have a crease running through the middle widthwise.

6 Halve the lemon, reserving one half and cutting the other half into thin slices. Place half the lemon slices and half the shallot slices just above the crease in the baking paper. Season a fish fillet to taste on both sides with sea salt and black pepper, then place on top of the lemons and shallots. Spoon over half the herb salsa, so it covers the fillet evenly, then place half the tomatoes on top. To seal the parcel, fold the baking paper over the fillet and crimp together by making repeated small folds around the edges. Place the parcel on a baking sheet and then repeat for the second fillet. Bake the fish in the oven for 15–20 minutes.

7 Once the potatoes are fork-tender, drain and return to the saucepan. Add the butter, stir through until melted, and season to taste if necessary. Mix the lavender through the potatoes and place a lid on the pan to keep them warm.

8 Check the fish is cooked by carefully opening one of the pouches and slicing into the fillet: if it looks opaque and flaky, then it's cooked.

9 Serve the fish en papillote with the potatoes, allowing diners to (carefully) cut into the parcels themselves to release the fragrant steam. Squeeze over the juice from the reserved lemon half and garnish with the fried capers.

SPICY BEEF LARB

1 tbsp uncooked sticky or basmati rice

2 echalion (banana) shallots, roughly chopped

4 lemongrass stalks (tough outer layers removed), roughly chopped

4 garlic cloves, roughly chopped

2 tbsps vegetable oil

1lb (450g) ground (minced) beef

1 tsp red pepper (dried chili) flakes

Large bunch of fresh mint, divided

Large bunch of cilantro (fresh coriander), divided

Large bunch of fresh Thai basil, divided

Juice of 1 lime

2 tbsps fish sauce

1½ tbsps jaggery, palm sugar, or dark brown sugar

1 tsp sriracha (optional)

Fine sea salt

Steamed rice and lime slices/wedges, plus bibb (round) or baby gem lettuce leaves (optional), to serve

SERVES 4 AS AN APPETIZER OR 2 AS A MAIN

Larb, sometimes written laab or laap, hails from Southeast Asia. At its simplest, larb consists of pan-fried ground (minced) meat mingled with chili peppers and toasted rice powder. It's often served with rice and fresh herbs, or wrapped in lettuce leaves. There are many iterations, with variations on the meat (from pork and chicken to duck and beef) and the aromatics; this one features the classic sweet-sour-umami trio of brown sugar, lime juice, and fish sauce, and hums with chili heat.

PAIR WITH A darker, malt-driven lager. An amber-hued maibock or märzen has enough sweetness and complexity to compete with the bold flavors in this dish, while still providing refreshment. You could also opt for a schwarzbier, whose roasty characteristics play well with the caramelized beef.

THREE BEERS TO TRY Köstritzer Schwarzbier (Germany); Reutberger Josefi-Bock (Germany); Uinta Baba Black Lager (US)

1 Toast the tablespoon of rice in a small skillet (frying pan) over medium-high heat, tossing frequently, for approximately 6–8 minutes, or until the rice is deep golden and smells nutty. Remove from the heat and let cool for several minutes. Transfer to a food processor or spice grinder, and grind finely. Transfer to a bowl and set aside.

2 Add the shallots, lemongrass, and garlic to a food processor. Pulse, pausing to scrape down the sides with a spatula, until the mixture is finely diced.

3 Add the vegetable oil to a large, heavy-bottomed skillet (frying pan)—preferably made from cast iron—and place over medium heat. Add the shallot mixture and cook, stirring frequently, for 4–5 minutes, or until it has softened, started to turn golden, and lost its raw aroma. Transfer to a bowl and set aside.

4 Wipe out the skillet and return to the stovetop over medium-high heat. Once the skillet is hot, add the beef. Break the beef up gently with a spatula and spread into a thin layer. Let cook undisturbed for 3–4 minutes, or until the beef is well browned on the bottom; season lightly with sea salt. Stir and redistribute the beef so that the pink parts are in direct contact with the skillet. Cook for a further 3 minutes or so, until the beef is well browned all over and cooked through.

5 Reduce the heat to the lowest setting, add the powdered rice and red pepper (dried chili) flakes to the beef, and toss lightly to combine. Scrape the shallot mixture into the beef, stir, and remove from the heat. Add half of each of the herbs and stir through.

6 Whisk the lime juice, fish sauce, and jaggery or sugar in a bowl. Pour over the beef and stir to coat. Season to taste with more sea salt and add the sriracha (if using).

7 Serve the larb on top of bowls of steamed rice, with the remainder of the fresh herbs and a slice or wedge of lime on the side. If you wish, you can also serve with a plate of bibb (round) or baby gem lettuce leaves, into which you scoop the larb mixture.

THYME AND LEMON FINANCIERS

1 stick (115g) unsalted butter, plus extra for greasing

2 tsps fresh thyme leaves, plus extra to garnish

¾ cup (170g) packed light brown sugar

½ cup (55g) finely ground almonds or almond flour

½ cup (70g) all-purpose (plain) flour

1 tsp fine sea salt

3 eggs, at room temperature

Zest of 1 lemon

MAKES 24

This recipe was inspired by the financiers I once ate years ago at Lyle's, one of London's best restaurants. Warm, fragrant with brown butter, and perfectly bite-sized, they were so delicious that I begged the kitchen for the recipe. Financiers are a classic French treat, made with finely ground nuts (usually almonds) and brown butter. Supposedly the name comes from the fact that they were favored by Paris's nattily dressed bankers, who appreciated their portability and the fact that they didn't leave stray crumbs on their suits. Classic financiers are baked in molds shaped like gold bars, but a miniature muffin pan (tin) works just as well.

PAIR WITH A dark, malty lager. A helles bock, with its golden body and lingering caramel sweetness, works well; a deeper, richer doppelbock is also an excellent pairing candidate and picks up the brown butter notes in the financiers.

THREE BEERS TO TRY Augustiner Maximator (Germany); Tegernseer Quirinus Dunkler Doppelbock (Germany); Tröegs Troegenator Double Bock (US)

1 Preheat the oven to 350°F/180°C/Gas 4. Use butter to thoroughly grease a mini muffin pan—ideally one that can hold 24 muffins—and set aside.

2 Brown the butter in a small saucepan over medium-high heat. As soon as the butter has melted, add the thyme leaves. Cook for 3–4 minutes, stirring frequently, or until the butter smells nutty and toasty, and has turned deep brown (watch constantly, as this can happen quickly and you don't want the butter to burn). Remove from the heat and immediately pour the thyme butter into a small bowl. Place in the freezer.

3 Mix the brown sugar, almonds (or almond flour), flour, and sea salt in a large mixing bowl, ensuring there are no lumps.

4 Separate the three eggs, adding the whites to a medium bowl and discarding the yolks (or saving them for another purpose). Whisk the egg whites until frothy—this will take about 45 seconds. Pour the egg whites into the dry mix, and fold to combine.

5 Remove the thyme butter mixture from the freezer (it will probably still be warm, which is fine); add to the batter, along with the lemon zest, and fold to combine.

6 Carefully spoon the batter (it will be quite thick and sticky) into the prepared muffin pan, filling each mold almost to the top. Bake for 12 minutes or until the financiers have risen and are deep golden. (Rotate the pan just over halfway through the cooking time if your oven has hotspots.) Remove the financiers from the oven and let cool in the pan for 5 minutes before transferring carefully to a cooling rack. Garnish each financier with a few thyme leaves. Store covered in the refrigerator for several days; the financiers also freeze well.

CHAI-SPICED CHEESECAKE

FOR THE FILLING

1½ cups (350ml) heavy (double) cream

2 tbsps high-quality, loose-leaf black tea or 2–3 teabags

2 tbsps vanilla paste or vanilla extract

1 tsp ground cinnamon

1 tsp ground cardamom

1 tsp ground ginger

1 tsp ground nutmeg

½ tsp ground cloves

9oz (250g) cream cheese

2 eggs

1 cup (200g) granulated sugar, divided

1¼ cups (300ml) sour cream

Freshly grated nutmeg

FOR THE CRUST

15 ginger snaps

2 tbsps packed light brown sugar

½ stick (55g) unsalted butter, melted

SERVES 8 TO 12

In my family, cheesecake is reserved for only the most special of occasions. This recipe, which originated with my grandmother, produces a cheesecake that's rich, creamy, and unbelievably decadent (no airy, New York-style cheesecakes allowed in my house). This contemporary twist adds tea-infused cream and aromatic spices, resulting in a fragrant, chai-spiced cheesecake that's worthy of all celebrations.

PAIR WITH A sweet, malty lager. A doppelbock, with its toffee-flavor notes and rich complexity, works well alongside the lush creaminess of this cheesecake and also complements its tea and spice notes. A rich, chocolatey Baltic porter also works well.

THREE BEERS TO TRY Ayinger Celebrator (Germany); Põhjala Öö Baltic Porter (Estonia); Sawmill Baltic Porter (New Zealand)

1 Ensure the heavy (double) cream, cream cheese, eggs, and sour cream are at room temperature. If they have been refrigerated, leave out for 2 hours before starting.

2 To make the tea-infused filling, heat the heavy cream in a small saucepan over low heat. Spoon the loose tea into a small piece of cheesecloth (muslin) or bouquet-garni bag, secure, and add to the cream. (Note: you can use teabags, but loose-leaf tea delivers a richer flavor.) Simmer the cream for 20–25 minutes, ensuring the mixture doesn't boil, or until it is a rich golden color and tastes strongly of tea. Remove and discard the tea bag(s), and pour the cream into a bowl. Let cool.

3 To prepare the crust, pulse the ginger snaps to a fine, sandy texture in a food processor. Alternatively, seal the ginger snaps in a Ziploc bag and crush gently with a rolling pin.

4 Mix the ginger-snap crumbs and brown sugar in a bowl. Add the melted butter and stir to combine. Transfer the crumb mixture to a 9- or 10-inch (23- or 25-cm) ceramic or Pyrex tart pan (dish). Press the crumbs evenly across the bottom and up the sides to form a crust. Set aside.

5 Preheat the oven to 350°F/180°C/Gas 4. Once the tea-flavored cream has cooled, add the vanilla flavoring and spices, and stir to combine.

6 Whip the softened cream cheese in a large bowl with a hand mixer or use a stand mixer. Add the eggs and ¾ cup (150g) of the sugar and beat well to combine, pausing to scrape down the sides of the bowl with a spatula. Add the tea-flavored cream and beat to combine. Pour the mixture into the prepared crust. Bake for 20–25 minutes, or until the filling is just set. Let cool for 1 hour on the countertop.

7 Add the sour cream and remaining ¼ cup (50g) sugar to a large bowl, beat well to combine, and pour over the cheesecake in a smooth layer. Top with the nutmeg, return the cheesecake to the oven, and bake for a further 10 minutes.

8 Remove the cheesecake from the oven and let cool to room temperature. Cover with plastic wrap (clingfilm) and chill in the fridge for 12–24 hours, or until fully set.

CHAPTER 3 | WHEAT BEERS

GUIDE TO WHEAT BEER STYLES BY JEN FERGUSON

When my partner Glenn and I first started dating in New Zealand, we would often meet up at the now long-gone Belgian beer café across the road from the radio station where he worked. We'd enjoy pots of mussels, fistfuls of frites dunked in mayonnaise, and huge, heavy pints of Hoegaarden, complete with a slice of lemon on top. They may not have transported Belgian culture halfway around the world terribly well, and they never did get those frites quite right, but the place did manage to instil in me a desire to try many more wheat beers (preferably without the lemon slice these days, please).

Wheat beers rock—from light and spicy witbiers and hefeweizens to rich dunkels and hoppy white IPAs, there truly is a wheat beer for everyone. (Tart Berliner weisses and goses are also technically wheat beers; read more about both in Chapter 1 Sours and Saisons, pages 18–49.)

In order to be called a wheat beer, a sizable proportion of a beer's grain bill must comprise—you guessed it—wheat (typically between 30–70 percent). Wheat contains more protein than barley, which helps to create the haze found in many wheat beers, as well as the smooth and silky mouthfeel and the gloriously thick heads for which they are also known.

Wheat beers are known above all else for flavor characteristics derived from esters and phenols—the fruity and spicy compounds produced by certain yeast strains during fermentation. In other styles of beer, estery and phenolic flavors and aromas might be considered off-notes, but here they are celebrated: banana, clove, citrus, and other yeast-produced aromatics add another dimension to wonderful wheats.

PALE WHEAT BEERS

Wine and food pairing expert Fiona Beckett describes pale wheat beers as "the beer world's equivalent of a crisp white wine" and, as far as generalizations go, it's a pretty good one. These styles are extraordinarily versatile and highly food-friendly.

Belgian witbiers, or bières blanches, are notable for their distinctly pale, hazy appearance—they contain a high proportion of wheat and are served unfiltered, with the yeast still present. Spicy and citrusy, these beers usually feature coriander and curaçao or orange peel, in addition to other spices.

German wheat beers, or weizenbiers/weissbiers, on the other hand, prominently feature yeast-produced banana esters and clove phenols, and are often quite crisp and dry. (As traditional German wheat beers typically fall under the Reinheitsgebot—the German Beer Purity law—they are not permitted to have additional spice or flavoring added.) Hefeweizen is unfiltered and cloudy (the prefix hefe means "with yeast"). Kristallweizen is the filtered version—as the name suggests, it's crystal-clear in appearance, with subtler banana and clove notes.

American-style wheat beers put a contemporary spin on the classic hefeweizen formula. Rather than using traditional German weizen yeast, brewers tend to use regular ale or lager strains. That means you're less likely to find the big banana, clove, or spicy notes the traditional yeasts provide; instead, American-style wheat beers primarily showcase intensely fruity, New World hop varieties.

DARK WHEAT BEERS

The two main styles of dark wheat beers—dunkelweizens and weizenbocks—both originally stem from Germany (southern Germany, to be precise).

Dunkelweizen is essentially a stronger, darker version of hefeweizen (dunkel is German for "dark"), thanks to the Vienna or Munich malts with which it's brewed. Dunkelweizens generally display the same clove and banana characteristics, but are much more toasty in flavor; banana bread is a great descriptor. Weizenbocks are stronger still—boozier, spicier, and fruitier, like a barley wine dressed in lederhosen.

WHITE IPA

White IPA is a terrific hybrid style, which, as its name suggests, brings together the refreshing spiciness of a Belgian wit with the big hop flavors of an IPA. The origin of this style is commonly attributed to both Kansas City's Boulevard Brewing and the Oregon-based Deschutes Brewery; the two created perhaps the world's first white IPA during a collaboration back in 2010. With Boulevard's passion for wheat beers and Deschutes' hop affinity, the solution must have seemed obvious: to combine both attributes in a single great beer.

Today, this style allows brewers to experiment with different adjuncts. Some of our favorite white IPAs contain decidedly nontraditional ingredients. Nanban Kanpai, for instance—a collaboration between the London-based Pressure Drop Brewery and chef Tim Anderson—showcases orange, grapefruit, and yuzu additions.

WHEAT WINE

Wheat wine has a lot in common with barley wine; the main difference is that it has a large percentage of wheat in the grist. Just like a barley wine, it's boozy, warming, and chewy, although generally a little drier. It's great with blue cheese and fruitcake, and makes a decadent accompaniment to rich food such as game.

A NEW TAKE ON TRADITION—
ALLAGASH BREWING, MAINE

In the US, Maine's Allagash Brewing has been getting American drinkers excited about wheat beers since 1995. It's a great example of how a new-world brewery is taking the traditions of an old-world brewery—in this case, Belgian—and creating its own unique beers.

Founder Rob Tod says, "As a Belgian-style brewery, that tradition has an enormous impact on how and what we brew. By one turn, Belgian-style brewing is bound by tradition—exemplified by styles like a tripel, witbier, or spontaneously fermented beer. On the other side, Belgium has beers that don't fall along any specific style guidelines. These beers use all sorts of ingredients like fruit, spices, sugar, oak barrels, and unique microbiota.

"This duality lets us enjoy the best of both worlds, from a brewing perspective. We get to brew our takes on very traditional styles, while also creating completely new beers that are guided only by what we think would taste great."

The brewery's iconic Allagash White is a Belgian-style witbier originally inspired by Rob's discovery and enjoyment of Hoegaarden in his early 20s. It's been hailed as one of the most important craft beers in America and, more than three decades later, it's still winning awards.

Rob says, "The witbier style is special because it's accessible to people who don't consider themselves 'beer fans' while also complex enough to satisfy someone who has been enjoying beer for years."

ESSENTIAL ALLAGASH BEERS

• Allagash White: Naturally! The beer, the legend...
• Odyssey: A dark wheat beer aged in oak barrels. Think treacle and dark fruits. Warming and incredibly special.

ROB'S PERFECT PAIRING

"Being from Maine, we have to say that our perfect pairing is boiled lobster and Allagash White. Both have flavors that are complex and subtle at the same time. When paired together, the citrus and spice in Allagash White is the perfect palate cleanser to the briny, sweet, and buttery flavor of a fresh lobster."

FOOD PAIRINGS

Wheat beers are some of the most flexible and versatile in the game. Lighter hefeweizens and witbiers are exceptional alongside shellfish, white fish, delicate herb salads, fruit dishes, fresh cheeses, and other subtly flavored foods that are overwhelmed by more potent styles. On the other hand, darker dunkelweizens do well with grilled meats, while the hoppiness of white IPAs cuts ably through fatty dishes. Then there's big and bold wheat wine, a natural pairing partner for the most robust meats and cheeses around.

STYLE	CHARACTERISTICS	PAIR WITH
Witbier	Pale, cloudy, citrus	Cucumber salad, ceviche, tuna steaks
Hefeweizen	Cloudy, banana, clove	Citrusy salads, fish and chips, pasta with ricotta
Kristallweizen	Clear, banana, clove	Fried squid with lemon aioli, sushi, delicate herb salads
American wheat beer	Hoppy, hazy, yeasty	Grilled white fish, quesadillas, paella
Dunkelweizen	Bready, golden, spicy	Duck salad, roasted cauliflower
Weizenbock	Malty, warming, spicy	Blondies, aged cheeses, plum tarts
White IPA	Hazy, hoppy, spicy	Salmon poke, avocado toast, braised chicken thighs
Wheat wine	Rich, warming, chewy	Blue cheese, game meats

SMASHED CUCUMBER SALAD

2 cucumbers (each weighing about 10oz/300g), washed and skin left on

1 tsp fine sea salt

Shichimi (Japanese spice blend) or red pepper (dried chili) flakes, to garnish

FOR THE MISO DRESSING

Thumb-sized piece of fresh ginger, peeled and finely chopped

1 garlic clove, finely chopped

Juice of 1 lemon

1½ tbsps white miso paste

1 tbsp tahini

2 tsps clear honey

1 tbsp Shaoxing rice wine

1 tbsp warm water

SERVES 4 AS A STARTER

Smashed cucumbers have long been enjoyed in Sichuan, but it would seem the wider world only woke up to the idea a few years ago. It's a simple but ingenious way to prepare this vegetable, which can often be watery and dull otherwise. By smashing a cucumber—and getting out some aggression simultaneously—and then salting it, it's as if you have completely changed its DNA. It becomes tender, but still has crunch; its craggy pieces hold sauce and flavor—it is simply infinitely better. Here, I serve the cucumber salad tossed with a quick miso dressing, for a dish that works well as a light summer salad or side dish.

PAIR WITH A citrusy wheat beer. Soft, frothy, and bright with citrus and herbaceous notes, witbiers work well with flavors that are fresh and not too bold. Grisettes, farmhouse-style beers made with malted wheat, are another good choice.

THREE BEERS TO TRY Burning Sky Blanche (UK); La Sirène Florette (Australia); St Bernardus Wit (Belgium)

1 Place one of the cucumbers on a cutting board. Use a rolling pin, the flat side of a heavy cleaver, or the bottom of a heavy pan to give the cucumber a few good whacks until smashed and broken into three or four large spears (be careful of flying seeds). Use a knife or your hands to cut or tear the spears into roughly 1-inch (2.5cm) pieces. Repeat for the second cucumber.

2 Add the cucumber pieces to a bowl, sprinkle over the sea salt, and stir to combine. Place in the refrigerator for 30 minutes.

3 Meanwhile, to make the miso dressing, mix the ginger, garlic, lemon juice, and miso paste in a small bowl. Add the tahini, honey, and rice wine, and whisk well. Add the warm water and whisk again until the dressing is smooth and quite thick. Set aside.

4 Remove the cucumber pieces from the refrigerator and use a sieve to strain off the water they've released, using the back of a spoon to press out any excess.

5 Transfer the cucumber to a serving bowl, add the dressing, and toss lightly to combine. Garnish with the shichimi or red pepper (dried chili) flakes and serve immediately.

TOMATO AND STRAWBERRY SALAD

¾ cup (100g) Marcona almonds

Large bunch of fresh basil (preferably purple basil)

5–6 heirloom tomatoes, sliced

7oz (200g) strawberries, hulled and cut into thin wedges

12 slices mojama or prosciutto

Small bunch of basil microgreens (optional)

Flaky sea salt (such as Maldon)

FOR THE DRESSING

⅓ cup (75ml) extra virgin olive oil

½ tbsp rice vinegar

Juice of 1 lemon

Large pinch of flaky sea salt

½ tsp freshly ground black pepper

SERVES 4 AS A STARTER OR 2 AS A MAIN

Tomatoes and strawberries—who would've thought? The love affair sounds unlikely, but it's only when you try the two ingredients together that you realize how harmonious the combination is. This recipe is my recreation of a summer salad I ate at a Spanish restaurant in London called Trangallán, which instantly alerted me to the pleasures of enjoying both red fruits side by side. It comes dressed with the simplest of vinaigrettes; translucent panes of mojama (Spanish cured tuna), toasted Marcona almonds, and two types of basil do the rest.

PAIR WITH A spice-led wheat beer. Recognizable for their hazy appearance and fluffy white heads, German-style weissbiers are gloriously refreshing. They're also rich in esters and phenols, which give them clove, banana, and even bubblegum flavors. Lean toward a spicy, clove-y wheat beer for this pairing, whether a classic German option or a modern take on the style.

THREE BEERS TO TRY Andechser Weissbier Hell (Germany); Bell's Brewery Oberon Ale (US); Cigar City Brewing Florida Cracker (US)

1 First make the dressing by adding all the ingredients to a small bowl and whisking well to emulsify. Set aside.

2 Toast the almonds in a small skillet (frying pan) over medium-high heat, tossing frequently, for 5–6 minutes, or until fragrant and golden brown. Remove from the heat and set aside.

3 To construct the salad, scatter some basil leaves across each plate. Divide the tomatoes and strawberries evenly between the plates, then top each salad with three or six slices of mojama or prosciutto (depending on whether you are serving the dish as a starter or main course).

4 Sprinkle the salads with the toasted almonds and basil microgreens (if using). Drizzle generously with the dressing and finish with a sprinkling of sea salt to taste.

FRIED SQUID WITH LEMON AIOLI

1lb (450g) small squid, cleaned and separated into bodies and tentacles

1 cup (250ml) whole milk

½ cup (25g) panko breadcrumbs

Heaping ½ cup (75g) all-purpose (plain) flour

½ tsp fine sea salt

1 tsp freshly ground black pepper

2 cups (500ml) vegetable oil

2 tbsps brined capers, rinsed and patted dry

Flaky sea salt (such as Maldon)

FOR THE LEMON AIOLI

2 garlic cloves, finely chopped

¾ tsp fine sea salt

1 egg yolk

¾ tsp Dijon mustard

6 tbsps (90ml) olive or vegetable oil

⅔ cup (150ml) extra virgin olive oil, divided

Juice and zest of 1 lemon, plus extra wedges to serve (optional)

SERVES 3 TO 4 AS A STARTER OR 2 AS A MAIN

During a recent trip to Sicily, I ate fried squid at a seaside market that was so good it stopped me in my tracks. So often calamari comes to the table soggy or rubbery; I couldn't believe I'd never had the good stuff before. Luckily, you don't have to book a trip to a Mediterranean idyll for a calamari fix—with just a few quick tricks, you can make Sicilian-grade fried squid at home. Marinating the squid in milk before frying it may sound strange, but it's a clever way of tenderizing it. Use a lemony aioli as a dipping sauce, and fry up some capers alongside for a zing of briny acidity.

PAIR WITH A kristallweizen. Named for its crystal clarity, this style of wheat beer is filtered, unlike hazy hefeweizen. With light, delicate flavors, kristallweizens serve up simple refreshment—and, in this case, cut through the oil and salt of the fried squid effortlessly. A modern wheat lager presents another good alternative.

THREE BEERS TO TRY Hofbräu München Kristall Weisse (Germany); Moa White Lager (New Zealand); Weihenstephaner Kristall Weissbier (Germany)

1 Ensure the squid is thoroughly cleaned and contains no grit (you can ask your fishmonger to do this for you). Place the tentacles in a bowl, removing and discarding any extra-long ones. Slice the main body of each squid into rings, about ½ inch (1cm) in diameter, and add to the bowl. Pour over the milk—the squid should be fully immersed. Cover and chill in the refrigerator for 1 hour.

2 Meanwhile, to make the aioli, use a mortar and pestle, or a food processor, to grind the garlic and sea salt into a paste. Whisk the egg yolk and mustard in a small bowl. Pour in the olive or vegetable oil in a very slow, steady stream, whisking constantly, until the mixture is very smooth and emulsified. Add half the extra virgin olive oil in the same way, then add the garlic paste and lemon zest and juice, and whisk well to combine. Continue adding the remaining extra virgin olive oil until the consistency of the aioli is to your liking. Cover and chill. You will probably have some aioli left over, but it keeps well in the refrigerator for several days.

3 Add the panko breadcrumbs to a spice grinder or food processor, and pulse until fine. Add the breadcrumbs to a bowl with the flour, sea salt, and black pepper, and mix well to combine. Remove the squid from the refrigerator.

4 Working in small batches, remove the squid from the milk, letting any excess drip off. Add to the flour mixture and use a fork to toss the squid gently until fully coated. Transfer the squid to a cutting board or plate. Repeat until all the squid pieces have been breaded. Discard the milk.

5 Pour the vegetable oil into a large, heavy-bottomed skillet (frying pan)—ideally made from cast iron—and heat on high until the oil reaches 350°F (180°C). The temperature will drop once the squid is added, so monitor this throughout the cooking process.

(Method continues overleaf)

6 Carefully add a small batch of squid to the hot oil, ensuring the skillet isn't too crowded, and cook for approximately 1 minute, using a slotted spoon or spider strainer to flip and rotate the pieces so they cook evenly (be careful, as the oil may spit). The squid should be crisp and golden brown after approximately 1 minute. Transfer the squid to a plate lined with paper towels and repeat for the remaining batches of squid.

7 Once all the squid is cooked, carefully add the capers to the oil and cook for just 45 seconds, or until they have opened and are very crisp. Remove from the oil and transfer to the plate with the squid.

8 Lightly season the squid and capers with sea salt and toss to combine. Divide between the plates and serve immediately, with a ramekin of the lemon aioli on the side and lemon wedges (optional).

SALMON POKE WITH MACADAMIA NUTS

½ cup (70g) macadamia nuts

7oz (200g) ripe pitted (stoned) mango, peeled and cut into ½-inch (1cm) cubes

1 small sweet onion, finely diced

2 scallions (spring onions), thinly sliced

1 bird's-eye chili pepper, finely chopped

1lb (450g) sushi-grade salmon fillet, skin removed and cut into ½-inch (1cm) cubes

1 tbsp toasted sesame oil

5 tsps soy sauce

1 tsp sesame seeds

Nori, sliced into thin strips

Steamed basmati or sushi rice, to serve (optional)

SERVES 4 AS
A STARTER OR
2 AS MAIN

Long before poke (pronounced poh-kay) was a fixture in trendy urban cafés aimed at clean-eaters and corporate workers after a light lunch, it was a staple of Hawaiian cuisine. Typically featuring fresh fish, seaweed, sweet onions, sesame oil, and soy sauce, poke is perfect warm-weather fare—no tropical beaches required. This version, inspired by Serious Eats, is based on the classic Hawaiian preparation, but also takes some liberties: I use salmon in place of the more traditional ahi tuna, trade candlenuts for macadamias, and add mango for a sweet and tropical contrast.

PAIR WITH A white IPA. With its rich umami flavors, plus the fattiness of the salmon, this dish can stand up to a bit of hopping. A white IPA—typically made with a heavy dose of wheat in the grain bill—is soft on the palate, fragrant with citrus notes, and a friend to seafood dishes.

THREE BEERS TO TRY Pressure Drop Nanban Kanpai White IPA (UK); Trillium Pier (US); Trzech Kumpli Pan IPAni (Poland)

1 Toast the macadamia nuts in a small skillet (frying pan) over medium-high heat, tossing frequently, for 5–6 minutes, or until golden brown. Let cool for a few minutes, then chop roughly and set aside.

2 Mix the mango, onion, scallions (spring onions), and chili pepper in a medium bowl.

3 Add the cubed salmon to the bowl, drizzle over the sesame oil and soy sauce, and add the sesame seeds. Add the cooled macadamia nuts. Stir well to ensure everything is thoroughly mixed and evenly coated. Garnish with the nori strips and let rest for 5–10 minutes.

4 Divide the salmon poke between bowls and serve immediately. If you want to make a heartier meal of this dish, then serve with steamed basmati or sushi rice.

SEA BASS CEVICHE

1 small sweet potato (about 7oz/200g), peeled and finely diced

½ red onion

1 ruby grapefruit

2 garlic cloves, finely chopped

1 bird's-eye chili pepper, finely chopped

Juice of 2 limes

1 tsp orange blossom water

2 boneless, skinless sea bass fillets (about 9oz/250g each)

1 large ripe avocado

Flaky sea salt (such as Maldon)

Small bunch of cilantro (fresh coriander), to garnish

SERVES 2

Think of ceviche as a balancing act between chili-pepper heat, citric acidity, and the freshness of the sea—when well made, this South American dish shimmers with bright, vibrant flavors. In this particular recipe, lime juice is used to "cook" delicate sea bass in a matter of minutes, while the merest dash of orange blossom water lends a just-perceptible floral note. Avocado and sweet potato add creaminess and richness, while red onion contributes just the right amount of crunch. When the weather is hot and you can hardly be bothered to cook, this is the dish to make.

PAIR WITH An orange- or grapefruit-infused wheat beer. This ceviche is made with both segments of ruby grapefruit and orange blossom water; a witbier, or similar style, that's been infused with additional citrus flavors brings out its bright fruity side.

THREE BEERS TO TRY Brew By Numbers Witbier Orange (UK); Modern Times Fortunate Islands—Grapefruit Zest (US); Schöfferhofer Grapefruit (Germany)

1 Cook the sweet potato in a saucepan of lightly salted boiling water for 10 minutes—you want the pieces to be fork-tender, but not mushy. Drain and set aside to cool to room temperature.

2 Thinly slice the red onion and add to a bowl of ice-cold water to reduce its intensity.

3 Use your sharpest knife to segment the grapefruit by slicing off the thick layer of peel and pith in long strips, from top to bottom, so only the fruit remains. Cut out the individual segments by slicing along the membranes to separate them (avoid adding the chewy, unpleasant membranes to the dish). Set the segments aside.

4 To make a marinade for the fish, combine the garlic, chili pepper, lime juice, and orange blossom water in a bowl, add ½ teaspoon of sea salt (or to taste), and set aside.

5 To prepare the fish, run your hands over both fillets to check for any lingering bones. Halve each fillet lengthwise and cut into roughly ½-inch (1cm) cubes. Add the fish to a small bowl and sprinkle over ½ teaspoon of sea salt, stirring gently to mix. Leave for 2 minutes before pouring over the lime juice mix. Stir gently to combine and return to the fridge for 15–20 minutes, after which the fish should be "cooked" and opaque.

6 Remove the fish from the refrigerator. Halve and pit (stone) the avocado, and cut a crosshatch into each half to dice. Scoop out the flesh and add to the fish.

7 Strain the onion slices and pat dry before adding to the fish with the sweet potato and grapefruit segments. Stir gently to combine and leave for 5 minutes for the flavors to intermingle before serving.

8 To serve, divide the ceviche between two plates or bowls, and finish with a garnish of cilantro (fresh coriander) and a sprinkle of sea salt.

SEARED DUCK SALAD WITH ORANGE VINAIGRETTE

2 duck breasts (about 6oz/170g each)

1½ tbsps olive oil

1 large onion, thinly sliced

1 cup (100g) walnut halves

7oz (200g) cherries, pitted (stoned) and halved

3½ oz (100g) baby-leaf spinach

Flaky sea salt (such as Maldon) and freshly ground black pepper

1 tbsp fresh thyme leaves, to garnish

FOR THE ORANGE VINAIGRETTE

2 garlic cloves, finely chopped

1½ tbsps red wine vinegar

2½ tbsps extra virgin olive oil

1 tbsp orange juice

1 tsp Dijon mustard

Zest of 1 orange

Large pinch of flaky sea salt

Freshly ground black pepper

SERVES 2

I don't know when duck salad became a staple of my kitchen repertoire, but I know why it did. Duck breast—especially when cooked so that its fat renders and its skin crisps—is the perfect weekday indulgence. This salad is also remarkably flexible; here, I serve the duck on spinach and pair it with wine-dark cherries, toasted walnuts, and seared onion, but you can also get creative with the results of a fridge forage. A basic vinaigrette, brightened here with orange juice, has enough acid to counterbalance the duck's fattiness and tie it all together.

PAIR WITH A dark, malty wheat beer. This dish brings a range of deep, rich flavors, from the browned onions and gamy duck to the mouth-staining cherries. Look for a beer with complementary richness and profundity, one that supplies its own decadence—a boozy wheat wine, say.

THREE BEERS TO TRY Brouwerij De Glazen Toren Jan De Lichte (Belgium); Erdinger Dunkel (Germany); Smuttynose Wheat Wine Ale (US)

1 Remove the duck breasts from the refrigerator about 20–30 minutes before cooking and pat dry with paper towels. Using a very sharp knife, cut a crosshatch pattern through the skin and fat layer on each breast, being careful not to slice into the meat below; this will help the fat render as it cooks. Season both sides generously with sea salt and black pepper. Set aside.

2 Add the olive oil to a large skillet (frying pan) and place over high heat. Add the onion once the oil is hot, but not smoking, and cook for 2–3 minutes, stirring frequently, until it begins to soften. Spread the onion in a thin layer and cook, without disturbing, for a further 2–3 minutes, or until starting to turn golden brown. Flip over and cook on the other side for several more minutes until golden brown on both sides. Remove from the heat and transfer to a bowl.

3 Toast the walnuts in a small skillet (frying pan) over medium heat for about 5–7 minutes, tossing frequently, until golden brown and fragrant. Set aside.

4 Just before you plan to cook the duck breasts, whisk all the ingredients for the vinaigrette in a bowl until well emulsified, and set aside.

5 Place the large skillet you used for the onion over high heat. When very hot, add the duck breasts, skin side down, and cook for 6 minutes, or until the skin has crisped and turned golden brown, and a great deal of fat has rendered out. As you cook, tilt the skillet frequently and use a small spoon to collect the rendered fat that pools at the bottom (save the fat in a small bowl, or discard). Press firmly on each breast with the back of a spoon to help render as much fat as possible—this results in a crisper skin.

(Method continues overleaf)

6 Flip the breasts over and cook for a further 3–4 minutes, depending on how well done you like your duck. Rotate the breasts frequently, so they cook evenly; you may want to use tongs to ensure they're evenly browned on all sides. Remove the skillet from the heat and transfer the breasts to a cutting board. Let rest for 5–10 minutes.

7 Meanwhile, construct the rest of the salad. Add the onion, walnuts, cherries, and spinach to a large bowl, pour over the dressing, and toss until everything is evenly coated. Divide the salad between two plates.

8 Slice the duck breasts thinly and arrange across the salads. Garnish with the thyme leaves and serve immediately.

SEARED TUNA STEAKS WITH BALSAMIC TOMATOES AND PADRÓN PEPPERS

6 medium vine tomatoes, removed from the stems and halved

About 2 tbsps olive oil, divided

1–2 tsps balsamic vinegar reduction

2 yellowfin tuna steaks (about 5oz/140g each)

7oz (200g) Padrón (or shishito) peppers

1–2 tsps extra virgin olive oil

½ lemon

Flaky sea salt (such as Maldon) and freshly ground black pepper

SERVES 2

In Barcelona's Barceloneta neighborhood, there is an arguably perfect bar and restaurant called El Vaso de Oro. It is narrow and thin, and contains one long bar which stretches the whole length of the room, behind which dapper men in white uniforms banter and take customers' orders. Beer is what you should order there, along with various grilled entrées, plates of tapas, and mounds of Russian salad. One of the best things I ate there was a seared tuna steak: seasoned with a crunch of salt and perfectly browned on the outside, it invariably came with roasted tomatoes and Padrón peppers. This simple recreation is very nearly as good.

PAIR WITH A coriander-driven witbier. Coriander is a traditional ingredient in Belgian witbiers, and it imparts a dry piquancy that's tremendously appealing. Against the simplicity of this dish, a witbier's subtle spicing could almost serve as a garnish.

THREE BEERS TO TRY Allagash White (US); Hitachino Nest White Ale (Japan); Northern Monk Bombay Dazzler (UK)

1 Preheat the broiler (grill) to a high heat. Arrange the tomatoes, cut sides down, on a baking sheet lined with foil. Drizzle with 1 teaspoon of the olive oil. Broil the tomatoes for approximately 5 minutes, or until they're steaming and starting to char. Remove the tomatoes from the broiler and flip over with tongs so the cut sides are facing upward. Drizzle over another teaspoon of olive oil, the balsamic vinegar reduction, and a sprinkle of sea salt. Broil the tomatoes for a further 5–6 minutes, or until browned on top and starting to fall apart. Remove from the broiler and set aside.

2 Meanwhile, pat the tuna steaks dry with paper towels and season on both sides with sea salt and black pepper. Set aside.

3 Add 1 tbsp of olive oil to a large skillet (frying pan) and place over high heat. When the oil is hot, add the Padrón or shishito peppers and cook, tossing frequently, for 6–7 minutes, or until blistered and darkened all over. Transfer the peppers and tomatoes to two serving plates.

4 Return the skillet to the stovetop and keep the heat on high. Add the tuna steaks once the skillet is very hot. If the steaks are on the thinner side (under about an inch/2.5cm thick), cook for 45 seconds before flipping and cooking for 30 seconds on the reverse. If the steaks are thicker, increase the cooking time slightly; tuna dries out easily and is best served rare, so don't worry too much about undercooking it.

5 Transfer the tuna steaks immediately to the plates, drizzle with a little extra virgin olive oil, and squeeze over the lemon. Lightly season the tuna, tomatoes, and peppers with sea salt, and serve at once.

CHICKEN POSOLE VERDE

1lb (450g) dried hominy

2 tbsps olive oil

2 large onions, thinly sliced

6 garlic cloves, finely chopped

1 tbsp cumin seeds

8 cups (2 liters) chicken stock

1¼ lb (600g) bone-in chicken thighs and drumsticks, skin removed

1lb (450g) tomatillos, husks removed and rinsed

2 jalapeños

2 poblano chili peppers (optional)

2 tsps Mexican oregano (or use regular oregano)

Fine sea salt and freshly ground black pepper

TO SERVE

1 red onion, thinly sliced

Small bunch of cilantro (fresh coriander)

Crumbled feta, queso fresco, or queso cotija

1 ripe avocado, peeled, pitted (stoned), and thinly sliced

Lime wedges

SERVES 8 TO 10

I first encountered posole—sometimes spelled pozole—on a long-ago trip to New Mexico. The dish, a hearty stew that hails from Mexico and the American Southwest, is wonderfully flexible: it can feature pork, chicken, or offal, or no meat at all, green tomatillos or fiery red chili peppers, and a host of optional toppings. The intrinsic, essential element of the dish is hominy: large, starchy kernels of corn that are soaked overnight and cooked until tender. Save this dish for a lazy Sunday when it can simmer for hours, and especially when you are craving comfort food.

PAIR WITH A hopped-up wheat beer. This verdant dish pops with brightness (lime and cilantro/fresh coriander) but also brings heartiness and heat to the table. A hoppy wheat beer has the softness to complement the citrus and zesty herbs, but also the backbone to help it stand up to the richer, more intense flavors.

THREE BEERS TO TRY Pivovar Raven White IPA (Czech Republic); Schneider Weisse Meine Hopfenweisse (Germany); Tired Hands We Are All Infinite Energy Vibrating at the Same Frequency (US)

1 The night before you plan to eat the posole, add the dried hominy to a large bowl and cover with double the volume of cold water. Let soak overnight.

2 The next day, prepare the posole. Heat the olive oil in a Dutch oven (or large saucepan with a lid) over medium-high heat. Add the onions and cook for 2–3 minutes, or until they start to soften. Season with sea salt and black pepper. Add the garlic and cook for a further 3–4 minutes, or until the onions are soft and the garlic has lost its raw aroma. Add the cumin seeds and cook for 1 minute more.

3 Drain the hominy and add to the Dutch oven with the chicken stock. Increase the heat to high and bring to a boil, then reduce to a simmer. Cover and cook for 1 hour.

4 Season the chicken thighs and drumsticks with sea salt and black pepper. Once the hominy has been cooking for 1 hour, add the chicken to the Dutch oven. Cover and simmer for about 40–45 minutes, or until the chicken is cooked through and beginning to fall from the bone.

5 Meanwhile, place the tomatillos, jalapeños, and poblano chili peppers (if using) on a baking sheet lined with foil. Broil (grill) on a high setting for 10–12 minutes, or until the vegetables are beginning to char. Flip the vegetables over and cook for a further 8–10 minutes, or until darkened on the other side and very soft. Remove from the broiler and let cool for 5 minutes. Transfer the tomatillos and any juices to a food processor.

6 Carefully slice the jalapeños and poblano chili peppers (if using) in half and remove the stems and seeds. (You can peel them too, if you wish.) Add to the food processor and blitz on high to make a loose sauce.

(Method continues overleaf)

7 Remove the chicken pieces from the Dutch oven and transfer to a plate until cool enough to handle. Remove the meat from the bones—discarding these and any gristly bits—and shred with your hands or a fork. Return the shredded chicken to the Dutch oven, add the tomatillo mixture and oregano, and stir well.

8 Cover and let cook for at least another 30 minutes. Taste for seasoning. If the mixture is quite watery, remove the lid and increase the heat to high to let it reduce slightly. The posole is done when the hominy kernels are completely tender and starting to burst.

9 When ready to serve, divide the posole between bowls. Serve with the red onion, cilantro (fresh coriander), and your choice of cheese, the avocado, and lime wedges, as preferred.

SPINACH GNUDI WITH CHESTNUTS AND MUSHROOMS

1 cup (235g) frozen spinach, defrosted

Scant 1 cup (215g) ricotta, drained of excess liquid

¾ cup (120g) finely grated Parmigiano Reggiano, plus extra to serve

3 egg yolks

½ tsp freshly grated nutmeg, plus extra to serve

1 tsp fine sea salt

½ tsp freshly ground black pepper

¾ cup (110g) 00-grade pasta flour, plus extra for dusting

¼ cup (40g) fine semolina

9oz (250g) chestnut mushrooms

2 tbsps olive oil

1¼ sticks (150g) butter

20–30 fresh sage leaves

5½ oz (150g) cooked and peeled chestnuts, chopped into large pieces

SERVES 4

Homemade pasta always sounds like an excessively difficult enterprise, but if you can whip up a batch of cookie dough, then you can make gnudi. These cheery little dumplings—often likened to ravioli filling—are made of ricotta and 00-grade flour, and just enough semolina to hold them together; you certainly don't need anything as advanced as a pasta roller to make them. In this recipe, the gnudi are made vibrant with spinach and spiced with nutmeg. Serve them with chestnuts and seared chestnut mushrooms, plus a snowfall of Parmigiano Reggiano, for a pleasingly autumnal preparation.

PAIR WITH A hefeweizen. With its hazy body, slightly creamy mouthfeel, and notes of banana esters, a traditional hefeweizen picks up the sweetness of the chestnuts and the spice notes of the nutmeg, and also matches the buttery richness of this dish.

THREE BEERS TO TRY Ayinger Bräuweisse (Germany); Lost and Grounded Cool Bananas (UK); Weihenstephaner Hefe Weissbier (Germany)

1 Line a baking sheet with parchment (baking) paper and sprinkle over some flour to prevent the gnudi sticking.

2 To make the gnudi, put the spinach in a sieve and press out any excess liquid with the back of a spoon. Transfer to a food processor, along with the ricotta, Parmigiano Reggiano, egg yolks, nutmeg, sea salt, and black pepper. Blend on high until the mixture is well mixed. Transfer to a large bowl.

3 Add the flour and semolina to the spinach mixture, and use a spoon or your hands to mix until the dough just comes together. Use a tablespoon to scoop out a small mound of dough. Roll the dough quickly into an even sphere between your palms; the gnudi should be about 1 inch (2.5cm) across, or the size of a large marble. Place the gnudi on the prepared baking sheet and repeat with the remainder of the dough. You should have about 30 gnudi. Cover loosely with plastic wrap (clingfilm), and rest for 10–15 minutes.

4 Meanwhile, prepare the chestnut mushrooms. Remove and discard the stems and use a paper towel to delicately brush off any dirt or grit from the caps; don't get the mushrooms wet, as they'll soak up the liquid and become soggy. Slice the mushrooms. Heat the olive oil in a heavy-bottomed skillet (frying pan)—preferably made from cast iron—over high heat until very hot, but not smoking. Add the mushrooms, spread out into an even layer, and cook without disturbing for 2–3 minutes, or until golden brown. (Depending on the size of the skillet, you may need to cook the mushrooms in two batches.) Flip the mushrooms over and cook on the other side for a further 2–3 minutes before transferring to a bowl and setting aside.

5 To cook the gnudi, bring a large saucepan of salted water to a boil, then reduce to a gentle simmer. Add one-third of the gnudi—work in batches, so the pot isn't overcrowded—and cook until they float to the surface of the water (about 4–5 minutes). Use a slotted spoon or spider strainer to transfer the cooked gnudi to a plate. Repeat for the remaining batches.

6 While the gnudi are cooking, melt the butter in a large skillet (frying pan) over medium-high heat and add the sage leaves in a single layer. Cook for 4–5 minutes, or until the butter has browned and the leaves are fried. Remove from the heat just as the butter begins to brown, so it doesn't burn. Add the mushrooms and chestnuts.

7 Transfer the gnudi to the skillet and gently ladle over the buttery mixture, ensuring they are evenly coated.

8 Divide the gnudi between the plates, sprinkle with freshly grated Parmigiano Reggiano and nutmeg, and serve immediately.

SHAWARMA-SPICED CAULIFLOWER WITH POMEGRANATE AND TAHINI SAUCE

1 large head of cauliflower, leaves and stem removed

4 garlic cloves, smashed

1 tsp coriander seeds

1 tsp cumin seeds

½ tsp caraway seeds

½ tsp ground allspice

½ tsp ground cinnamon

½ tsp ground cardamom

¼ tsp ground turmeric

¼ tsp smoked paprika

¼ tsp hot chili powder

3 tbsps olive oil

½ tsp fine sea salt

FOR THE TAHINI SAUCE

2 tbsps tahini (look for high-quality tahini with a runny consistency)

3 tbsps Greek yogurt

Juice of ½ lemon

1 garlic clove, finely chopped

Pinch of fine sea salt

2 tbsps cold water

Freshly ground black pepper

TO SERVE

4–6 pitas, warmed briefly in the oven (optional)

Drizzle of pomegranate molasses

Ground sumac

Small bunch of fresh mint leaves, torn

Small bunch of fresh flat-leaf parsley, torn

1 tbsp pomegranate seeds

1 red onion, sliced (optional)

SERVES 2

Cauliflower is ubiquitous on restaurant menus and on Instagram; so much so that I hesitate to admit before the cauliflower brigade that it took me a long time to warm up to this vegetable. My stance only changed when I visited Berber & Q, a Middle Eastern restaurant in London that serves its cauliflower shawarma-style: coated in spices, roasted whole, and then anointed with pomegranate and rose petals. It's a wildly good dish, but slightly tricky to replicate at home where you probably don't have a large and fiery grill. This recipe simplifies the dish for a home kitchen, making it oven-ready and adding a bit of richness in the form of tahini sauce.

PAIR WITH A dunkelweizen. Darker than a hefeweizen, this in-between style of wheat beer is amber in hue and features a delicate, caramelized sweetness, ample spice notes, and a pleasingly toasty profile. It's still quenching and refreshing, but can hold its own against deeper, spicier flavors.

THREE BEERS TO TRY Ayinger Urweisse (Germany); Dogfish Head Carobock (US); ParrotDog RareBird: Tieke (New Zealand)

1 Preheat the oven to 400°F/200°C/Gas 6. Line a baking tray with foil.

2 Use your hands to snap off individual cauliflower florets until the entire head has been broken down, halving any particularly large florets. Rinse and pat dry with paper towels. Transfer the florets to a large bowl and add the garlic.

3 To prepare the spices, add the coriander, cumin, and caraway seeds to a spice grinder or mortar and pestle, and grind finely. Add the ground spices to a ramekin or small bowl along with the remaining spices, and mix to combine.

4 Drizzle the olive oil over the cauliflower and garlic, then sprinkle with the spice blend and sea salt. Toss well, using a spoon or your hands to ensure the florets are evenly coated. Transfer to the prepared baking tray and spread out in a single layer.

5 Roast the cauliflower for 30–40 minutes, or until completely tender and browned on the edges, pausing halfway through the roasting time to rotate and flip the florets.

6 Meanwhile, to prepare the tahini sauce, mix the tahini, Greek yogurt, lemon juice, garlic, and sea salt in a small bowl. Add the water and whisk to form a sauce with a pourable consistency; you can add slightly more water if you prefer your sauce thinner. Season to taste and set aside.

7 Once the cauliflower is cooked, divide between two plates, or serve on top of fluffy pieces of warm pita (if using). Top with the tahini sauce—you may not need all of it—and a drizzle of pomegranate molasses. Garnish with a sprinkle of sumac, the torn mint and parsley leaves, a tablespoon of pomegranate seeds, and red onion slices (if using).

BLONDIES WITH SWEET POTATO RIPPLE

2 sticks (225g) unsalted butter, cubed

1⅔ cups (350g) packed light brown sugar

2 eggs

2 tsps vanilla extract

2 tsps ground cardamom

1½ tsps fine sea salt

2¼ cups (280g) all-purpose (plain) flour

3½ oz (100g) chocolate chips

Pinch of flaky sea salt, such as Maldon (optional)

FOR THE SWEET POTATO RIPPLE

¾ cup (200g) canned sweet potato purée (or use pumpkin purée)

⅓ cup (70g) packed light brown sugar

1 tsp vanilla extract

MAKES 12 LARGE BLONDIES

It may sound sacrilegious, but I've never loved brownies as much as one is supposed to—they're too rich for me. Blondies, on the other hand—which I'd describe as similar to chocolate-chip cookies, but thick and fudgy—were a staple of my childhood that I still adore. It helps that they're made with near-obscene amounts of butter; it also helps that, as in this recipe, they're perfumed with ground cardamom, topped with a crunch of sea salt, and drizzled with a ripple of sweet potato.

PAIR WITH A sweet, dark wheat beer. I love the rich, beguiling complexity of these beers, which taste like caramel and plums soaked in syrup and dates, warm wood and spices. High in alcohol, pleasantly sweet, dessert-like in their own right, they're just the thing for an indulgence of this caliber.

THREE BEERS TO TRY Schneider Weisse Mein Aventinus (Germany); The Bruery White Chocolate Wheat Wine (US); Leavenworth Biers Boulder Bend Dark Wheat Ale (US)

1 Preheat the oven to 350°F/180°C/Gas 4. Line a 9 x 12-in (23 x 30cm) baking pan (tin) with parchment (baking) paper, ensuring it is big enough to cover all four sides.

2 To make the sweet potato ripple, add the sweet potato (or pumpkin) purée to a small saucepan with the sugar. Cook over medium-high heat for 4–5 minutes, stirring frequently, until the mixture reduces and thickens. Remove from the heat. Add the vanilla extract, stir to combine, and transfer to a bowl to cool.

3 To make the blondie batter, melt the butter in a saucepan over medium-high heat. Once the butter has completely melted, cook for 3–5 minutes. The butter will foam up; stir very frequently until it has changed to a deep amber color and smells nutty. Take off the heat and transfer immediately to a large mixing bowl. Cool for 5–10 minutes.

4 Add the sugar to the cooled butter and beat with a hand mixer on low until well combined. Add the eggs, vanilla extract, cardamom, and sea salt, and beat to combine, pausing to scrape down the sides of the bowl with a spatula. Add the flour and beat on low until just combined. Add the chocolate chips and stir through with a spoon.

5 Scrape the blondie batter into the prepared baking pan and press into an even layer, ensuring the baking paper doesn't move out of place. Drizzle the ripple over the batter and use the back of a spoon to swirl it over the surface and create small divots in which it can pool. Finish with a sprinkle of sea salt for added crunch, if you wish.

6 Bake the blondies for 30–35 minutes (or for several minutes longer if your pan is smaller and your blondies are thicker). Let cool and set completely in the pan. These blondies are on the underbaked side and fudgy in texture, so need time to set properly.

7 Once the blondies are completely cooled, remove from the pan by grasping the baking paper, lifting out the entire parcel, and transferring to a cutting board. Peel off the baking paper and slice into even squares. You can store the blondies in an airtight container at room temperature for up to 3–4 days.

DUTCH BABY PANCAKE, STRAWBERRY COMPOTE, AND WHIPPED BASIL CREAM

3 tbsps (45g) unsalted butter, divided

3 eggs, at room temperature

¾ cup (175ml) whole milk, at room temperature

Heaping ½ cup (75g) all-purpose (plain) flour

Pinch of fine sea salt

Zest of 1 lemon

1½ tbsps granulated sugar

1 tsp vanilla extract

FOR THE WHIPPED BASIL CREAM

1¼ cups (300ml) heavy (double) cream

Large bunch of fresh basil leaves, roughly chopped, plus extra to garnish

Zest of 1 lemon

2 tbsps granulated sugar

FOR THE STRAWBERRY COMPOTE

9oz (250g) strawberries, hulled and sliced into thin wedges (reserve a few wedges to garnish)

2–3 tbsps granulated sugar

1 tbsp lemon juice

1 tsp ground tonka bean (or use ½ tsp ground cinnamon and ½ tsp almond extract)

SERVES 2

Tell friends you ate a Dutch baby and they'll understandably raise an eyebrow. But once they hear Dutch babies are effectively plate-sized Yorkshire puddings, crisp at the edges and tender within, opinions might change. Dutch babies work equally well in sweet or savory contexts. Here, I accompany the pancake with a spiced strawberry compote and lightly sweetened, basil-infused whipped cream.

PAIR WITH A fruity wheat beer with some sweetness of its own. Playful, light, and drinkable from 11am, this beer should be a welcome staple of lazy weekend mornings.

THREE BEERS TO TRY 21st Amendment Hell or High Watermelon (US); Schlafly Raspberry Hefeweizen (US); Two Roads Road Jam (US)

1 To make the basil cream, add the heavy (double) cream, chopped basil, and lemon zest to a small saucepan and place over medium heat. Cook for 5 minutes until the cream is hot, starting to steam, and small bubbles form at the edges of the pan (don't let the cream boil). Remove from the heat and transfer to a bowl. Let cool for 5 minutes, cover, and chill for at least 2 hours until the cream is very cold. (To speed up the process, place the cream in the freezer, but check frequently to ensure it doesn't freeze.)

2 To make the compote, cook the strawberries in a small saucepan with the sugar, lemon juice, and tonka bean (or cinnamon and almond extract) on medium-high heat for 7–10 minutes, or until the strawberries have broken down and the compote has the texture of thick jam. Transfer to a bowl and let cool for 5 minutes, then cover and chill.

3 Once the basil cream has chilled for 1½ hours and is nearly ready to whip, make the pancake batter. Heat a cast iron skillet for 30 minutes in the oven at 450°F/230°C/Gas 8.

4 Melt 2 tablespoons (30g) of the butter in a small saucepan and set aside to cool for a few minutes. Beat the eggs in a blender or food processor on high speed for around 1 minute. Reduce the speed to low and add the milk followed by the melted butter with the motor still running. Pause, add the flour, sea salt, lemon zest, sugar, and vanilla extract, and blend until just combined. Rest the batter for 10–15 minutes.

5 Remove the hot skillet from the oven. Add the last tablespoon (15g) of butter, which should melt immediately, and swirl to coat the skillet. Pour in the batter and return the skillet to the oven immediately. Bake the Dutch baby for 15–20 minutes, or until puffed up, golden, and browned at the edges. Remove from the oven and let cool for 5 minutes.

6 Meanwhile, remove the cream from the refrigerator/freezer (it must be very cold to whip properly). Strain off the basil leaves and return the cream to the chilled bowl. Start beating the cream with a hand mixer, slowly adding the sugar as you beat, to help the cream stabilize. Beat for 3–4 minutes, until soft peaks form.

7 Top the pancake with the compote, cream, reserved strawberries, and basil, then serve.

CHAPTER 4 | PALES, IPAS, AND DIPAS

GUIDE TO PALE, IPA, AND DIPA STYLES BY JEN FERGUSON

Hops, hops, hops—the supermodels of the craft beer world, where just their names alone on the front of a can or keg badge are enough to cause a frenzy. Poor old malt and yeast can only dream of one day achieving such glory.

We've got the Americans to thank for the dominance of hops. When craft beer first became a "thing" back in the 1970s and 1980s, with the emergence of beers such as Anchor Liberty Ale, Samuel Adams Boston Lager, and Sierra Nevada Pale Ale, it was the prominent use of hops—in particular the newly developed, resinous hop varieties from the Pacific Northwest, such as Cascade—that set the burgeoning scene apart. Now, pales and IPAs are among the most popular styles in the craft beer world, and huge efforts are being made by hop companies to develop exciting new strains and, hopefully, discover the next super-hop. Check out our Key Hop Varieties (see pages 15–16) if you haven't already. We heart hops.

If you're reading this book, you probably already know the general difference between hoppy styles like pale ales, IPAs, and double IPAs, but for avoidance of doubt, here's a quick guide. In a nutshell, the distinctions between styles largely come down to strength: both in terms of ABV and boldness of flavor. A pale ale or session IPA will generally clock in between 4–6% ABV, although a session IPA tends to be hoppier and less malt-driven than a pale ale (American pale ales, or APAs, made with significant quantities of US hops, are an exception). Amber ales are a variation on pale ales, and feature a bigger malt backbone. IPAs are bolder in flavor and also stronger, usually between 5.5–7.5% ABV. Double IPAs (DIPAs) and triple IPAs (TIPAs) are stronger still, with ABVs of around 8–10% and 10%-plus, respectively. Both tend to be sweeter and stickier due to the additional malt content, which helps boost their ABVs.

Within these key types, there are many sub-styles, all with very different flavor profiles. Of course, the speed at which trends develop in craft beer means by the time you read this, there'll probably be a dozen more IPA styles that haven't even been invented yet. For now, though, here are some of the most popular.

EAST COAST VS WEST COAST VS SAN FRANCISCO

Until recently, if you drank an American-style pale ale or IPA, it would probably taste like resinous hops, with ample notes of dank citrus, tropical fruits, and pine, plus bracing bitterness. For a long time, bitterness was the IPA's X-factor, and brewers sought to outdo each other by making ever more eye-watering takes on the style. These hopped-up IBU bombs are today known as West Coast IPAs, and they pretty much had the market cornered… until the East Coast struck back a couple of years ago with the craze for haze.

The East Coast IPA—also known as the New England IPA (NEIPA) or Vermont IPA—is everything the West Coast IPA is not. It's cloudy rather than clear, soft as opposed to sticky, sweet instead of bitter, fruity over resinous. Brewers use techniques such as dry hopping (adding extra hops during fermentation and conditioning) to pack in as much flavor and aroma as possible. They also use lower-attenuating yeast strains so that more residual sugars remain in the beer, and add ample quantities of wheat and oats to produce that famously hazy, juice-like appearance.

The East Coast-style now extends to pales, DIPAs, and even TIPAs. It's exciting to see these incredibly drinkable hoppy styles ushering in a new generation of beer drinkers who might otherwise have been put off by high levels of bitterness. The juice is loose, you might say.

Even newer to the scene are Brut IPAs, which originated in the San Francisco Bay area in early 2018 and instigated a rush from breweries all around the world to jump on the bandwagon. Brut IPAs are pale, incredibly dry, and highly effervescent, like champagne, but still full of abundant hop aromatics. Their dryness is achieved via an enzyme (amyloglucosidase) that is usually used to reduce the sweetness of big, saccharine beers, such as imperial stouts or double and triple IPAs. Will the Brut IPA stick around? Despite the hype, I for one hope so—it's a terrifically refreshing style which lends itself so well to dishes such as sushi, tacos, and grilled fish.

WHITE, BLACK, AND RED HOPPY STYLES

There's more to these variations on the IPA than simply their color. White IPAs are made with wheat and are typically a wonderful marriage of the hoppiness of an IPA, plus Belgian witbier spices, and are often fermented with witbier yeast. Black IPAs, on the other hand, are hopped-up, bitter beers made with dark malts, similar if not identical to hoppy porters. Red ales and IPAs, meanwhile, are hop-forward beers made with darker malts that add a caramel color and some sweetness—a little bit like an IPA crossed with an amber ale. You'll also see rye IPAs on the shelf. These IPAs are made with significant quantities of rye malt, which adds an earthy, peppery spiciness to the beer.

OTHER INTERNATIONAL STYLES

I might be biased, having grown up there, but some of the finest hoppy beers in the world hail from New Zealand. Kiwi pales and IPAs are similar in many ways to US styles, but have a distinct character all of their own, thanks to the use of New Zealand hops (which are some of the most sought-after on the planet). Varieties such as Motueka, Wai-iti, and the coveted Nelson Sauvin, are highly aromatic due to extremely high percentages of essential oils, and give forth huge citrus, floral, and tropical-fruit flavors. Nelson Sauvin, in particular, imparts a lush bouquet of melon, gooseberry, and white-wine characteristics.

Hop (ahem) to the other side of the world and you'll find English pales and IPAs, beers that use indigenous English ingredients (and which represent the origins of these popular styles). These days, English hops get something of a bad rap for tasting a bit twiggy and dull. However, they can lend subtle spiciness, plus herbal, marmalade, and earthy notes to certain beers, especially more malty styles like amber ales. And, as temperatures increase and growing conditions evolve due to climate change, new, fruiter strains of English hops, such as Jester, are starting to gain some momentum.

Finally, let's hear it for Belgian pale ales and IPAs. We've included these styles in this chapter, though their hop character can be somewhat muted in favor of their biscuity malt character and spicy Belgian yeast. Brasserie de la Senne's Taras Boulba is my go-to Belgian pale if I want a refreshing citrus hit, and I always have a bottle of "emergency Orval" in the fridge, just in case a hangover cure is needed.

THE CULT OF THE HOP—GARAGE PROJECT, WELLINGTON, AND CLOUDWATER, MANCHESTER

Of all the beers out there, hoppy styles are usually the ones that have customers lining up around the block—just look to the likes of Treehouse, Trillium, and Other Half in the US. Breweries that nail the art of the hop quickly develop a cult following, as has been the case for New Zealand's Garage Project and the UK's Cloudwater Brew Co. Both breweries' outputs cover a huge range of styles, but it's their hoppy beers that have achieved the status of legend. Garage Project's multi-award-winning Pernicious Weed IPA and Cloudwater's coveted DIPAs are both enormously popular.

Part of the fascination for drinkers is the incredible versatility that hops possess. As Garage Project's head brewer Pete Gillespie explains, "Hops offer so many different flavors that the various combinations feel like they are endless. As a brewer, I feel like I'm still learning new things about hops and how best to use them."

Paul Jones (below), co-founder of Cloudwater, agrees. "Hops can taste like everything, from grassy dill and cumin to bright passion fruit and pineapple, but the specific aromas and flavor combinations from hops aren't something you can encounter anywhere else. I dearly love wine, cocktails, sherry, sake, and many other types of alcohol, but there's simply nothing out there that matches the flavor and impact of an excellent hoppy beer."

Both look forward to continuing to push the boundaries of beer further. "Inspiration can come from anywhere," Pete says. "Our beers have been inspired by everything, from the movie *Apocalypse Now*, Japanese dashi broth, the legendary animosity between Biggie and Tupac, the ballet, to a famous batch of acid from the '60s… When inspiration strikes, mash in."

ESSENTIAL GARAGE PROJECT BEERS

• Pernicious Weed Imperial IPA: An unapologetic love letter to New Zealand hops. Humulus lupulus—specifically Rakau and Nelson Sauvin—features center stage in this dank, sticky, bitter DIPA.
• Party & Bullshit IPA: GP goes East. A hazy, cloudy tribute to the New England style that serves up tropical juice while retaining balanced bitterness.

PETE'S PERFECT PAIRING

"Hoppy beer is great with anything fatty or greasy. It just cuts through the grease and refreshes the palate so well. We sponsor Burger Wellington, a local burger and beer-matching competition that runs throughout August. The winning combination uses an IPA more often than not, and for good reason."

ESSENTIAL CLOUDWATER BEERS

• Small Pale (hops vary): The Cloudwater team change their hops more often than their underpants, so finding the same hop combination twice can be a bit like winning a line in bingo. All the Small Pales to date have been terrific—with heaps of flavor and just 2.9% ABV.
• DDH IPA Citra BBC: An absolute juice monster that showcases the wonder that is the Citra hop.

PAUL'S PERFECT PAIRING

"Jetty or Kook IPA with a basket of wings and a slice of pizza at San Diego's Pizza Port, or pints of Tegernseer Hell with sausages, or a pile of crispy tempura with a delicate lager. As far as food and drink pairings go, I'm a big fan of drinking what's freshest and most delicious wherever I am, with the local delicacy or specialty."

FOOD PAIRINGS

Pairing food with hoppy beers can present an interesting challenge for the home cook. Some hoppy beer styles can be so bitter that they totally overwhelm gentler flavors. Others feature such vibrant hop aromatics that it's tricky to find a dish that can hold its own. As a general approach, it's worth letting the beer lead you. Hops are excellent at cutting through salt and tempering fat; look to fried and grilled meats, burgers, oily fish like salmon, and other dishes that could use with a counterbalancing effect. You might also take inspiration from the hop strains themselves: a beer made with tropical Citra is a dream alongside a shrimp (prawn) and mango curry, for instance. West Coast IPAs—both resinously bitter but somewhat sweet, thanks to the caramel malt present—pair surprisingly well with umami flavors, as well as carrot cake.

STYLE	CHARACTERISTICS	PAIR WITH
Pale and session IPA		
Pale	Hoppy, malty, balanced	Dal and rice, cheeseburger, chicken wings
Session IPA	Lower ABV, hoppy, bitter	Fried chicken, pork tacos, pad see ew
IPA		
West Coast	Dank, resinous, bitter	Steak, mushroom pasta, carrot cake
East Coast	Soft, hazy, juicy	Shrimp and mango curry, falafel gyros, nectarine burrata salad
Brut	Dry, fruity, effervescent	Lemon tart, chèvre chaud salad, grilled salmon
Belgian	Spicy, dry, hoppy	Aged cheeses, chicken tikka
White	Hazy, hoppy, spicy	Lemon risotto, moules frites
Black	Dark, hoppy, lightly roasty	Chili, cured salami, barbecued meat
Double IPA	Hoppy, boozy, sweet	Lamb chops, barbecued brisket
Triple IPA	Even hoppier, boozier, sweeter	Pungent cheeses, game meat

NECTARINE PANZANELLA SALAD WITH CROUTONS

1 small red onion, thinly sliced

2½ oz (70g) arugula (rocket)

2 ripe nectarines, pitted (stoned) and thinly sliced

9½ oz (270g) cherry tomatoes, halved

Small bunch of fresh tarragon leaves, chopped

1 large burrata

8–12 slices prosciutto

Flaky sea salt (such as Maldon)

Small handful of toasted coconut flakes, to serve

FOR THE CROUTONS

1 tbsp (15g) unsalted butter

1 tbsp olive oil

6–8 x 1-inch (2.5cm) slices of stale baguette

1 garlic clove, peeled

Flaky sea salt and freshly ground black pepper

FOR THE DRESSING

1 tbsp white wine vinegar

2 tbsps lemon juice

2 tbsps extra virgin olive oil

2 tbsps orange-infused or regular olive oil

Pinch of flaky sea salt

Freshly ground black pepper

SERVES 4 AS A STARTER OR 2 AS A MAIN

Panzanella salad first emerged in Tuscany as a canny way to use up stale bread; these days, it's a staple of summertime eating—fresh, but still hearty enough to enjoy as a meal on its own. Though the classic panzanella features tomatoes and basil, I like it even better with perfectly ripe nectarines, which are especially good counterposed with nuggets of burrata and aged prosciutto. Top your salad with toasted coconut flakes for an added dose of sunny sweetness.

PAIR WITH A fruity IPA with lactose. Often described as milkshake or ice-cream IPAs, these beers are known for their pillowy softness in the mouth, creamy appearance, and sweet, often fruit-led, flavor profiles. Here, they should pick up the ripe nectarines as well as the burrata.

THREE BEERS TO TRY Naparbier Milky Brain Milkshake IPA (Spain); WeldWerks Fruity Bits—Piña Colada (US); Whiplash Scaldy Split Ice Cream IPA (Ireland)

1 First, make the croutons. Heat the butter and olive oil in a large skillet (frying pan) over medium-high heat until hot. Add the slices of bread and cook on one side for approximately 3 minutes, or until golden brown. Flip the slices and season lightly with sea salt and black pepper, then cook for a further 2–3 minutes, or until golden brown on both sides.

2 Remove the skillet from the heat and transfer the bread to a cutting board. Let cool for several minutes until safe to handle. Rub the garlic clove over both sides of each slice (you probably won't use the whole clove). Slice the bread into cubes and set aside.

3 Next, prepare the dressing by whisking all the ingredients together in a small bowl until emulsified. Set aside.

4 To make the salad, place the onion in a bowl of cold water and let sit for 10 minutes, to help cut down the pungency.

5 Meanwhile, add the arugula (rocket), nectarines, tomatoes, tarragon, and croutons to a large bowl. Drizzle over most of the dressing and toss to coat. Leave for a few minutes to allow the flavors to infuse.

6 Take the onion out of the bowl, dry with paper towels, and add to the salad. Toss to coat.

7 Divide the salad between the plates. If the burrata has been sitting in liquid, drain briefly, then tear roughly into gloopy pieces and divide between the salads. Allocate 2–3 pieces (4–6 pieces for a main course) of prosciutto per person, tear roughly, and share between the salads.

8 Drizzle the salads with the remaining dressing. Finish with a final seasoning of sea salt and a sprinkle of toasted coconut flakes. Serve immediately.

FRIED AVOCADO WEDGES

1 large, just-ripe avocado

½ cup (70g) all-purpose (plain) flour

½ tsp fine sea salt

½ tsp hot chili powder

½ tsp onion or garlic powder

½ tsp freshly ground black pepper

½ tsp paprika

2 eggs

½ cup (30g) panko breadcrumbs

3 tbsps nutritional yeast (optional)

2 cups (500ml) vegetable oil

FOR THE DIPPING SAUCE

½ cup (115g) thick Greek yogurt (such as Fage)

½ tsp fine sea salt

2 tbsps extra virgin olive oil

1 tsp Dijon mustard

1 tsp lime juice

Pinch of granulated sugar

Large bunch of cilantro (fresh coriander)

SERVES 2

I first encountered fried avocados at a taqueria in Brooklyn called Güeros, where they were served inside an irresistibly good taco. This is a snacky take on fried avocados: coated with crunchy panko breadcrumbs and creamy on the inside, they take minutes to fry up. For a dipping sauce, I wanted something akin to mayonnaise, but without the egginess; instead, I used Greek yogurt and added mustard, olive oil, lime juice, and enough cilantro (fresh coriander) to turn it a cheery shade of green.

PAIR WITH A crisp pale ale or session IPA. This recipe is flexible enough to work with a wide array of hoppy styles, but a pale ale or session IPA with a pithy, citrusy character and lightly bitter finish will help cut through the avocado's richness.

THREE BEERS TO TRY Burnt Mill Pintle Pale Ale (UK); Fork Brewing Godzone Beat (NZ); Half Acre Daisy Cutter (US)

1 To make the wedges, use a knife to halve and pit (stone) the avocado. Leaving the peel on, run the knife the length of the avocado in ½-inch (1cm) slices. Use a spoon to gently scoop out the wedges and separate them. Repeat for the other avocado half.

2 Add the flour, sea salt, chili powder, onion/garlic powder, black pepper, and paprika to a bowl, and stir well to combine. Beat the eggs in another small bowl. Add the breadcrumbs and nutritional yeast (if using) to a third small bowl, and mix to combine.

3 Line a plate or small tray with foil and begin battering the wedges. Place the first wedge in the flour and toss lightly to coat. Transfer to the bowl of beaten eggs and use a fork to carefully dredge and flip the wedge until it is coated in egg. Let any excess batter drip off before transferring to the bowl of breadcrumbs and tossing until completely coated. Place the wedge on the prepared plate or tray, and repeat for the remaining wedges. Place the wedges in the refrigerator for 15–20 minutes to set.

4 Meanwhile, to prepare the dipping sauce, blend the yogurt, sea salt, and olive oil in a food processor on high until smooth and whipped. With the motor running, add the Dijon mustard, lime juice, sugar, and cilantro (fresh coriander). Continue to blend until the sauce is smooth and uniform. Set aside.

5 Next, fry the wedges. Place a large, heavy-bottomed skillet (frying pan)—ideally cast iron—over high heat and add the vegetable oil. Heat the oil for about 4–5 minutes, or use a cooking thermometer to check it has reached a temperature of 350°F (180°C). Add one wedge to the oil to test; it should immediately bubble vigorously. Fry for 1 minute, flipping and rotating with tongs, until the wedge is crisp and deep golden brown all over. Transfer to a plate lined with paper towels. Repeat for the other wedges—depending on the size of the skillet, you will probably have to cook the wedges in 3 or 4 batches to avoid overcrowding—and monitor the oil temperature as you go.

6 Transfer the dipping sauce to a small bowl or ramekin, and serve immediately with the fried avocado wedges.

DAL WITH FRIED ONIONS AND LIME CREAM

1¼ cups (250g) chana dal (or use yellow split peas)

About 4 tbsps (60g) unsalted butter

1 large onion, finely diced

5 large garlic cloves, finely chopped

Thumb-sized piece of fresh ginger, peeled and finely chopped

2 bird's-eye chili peppers, finely chopped

2 tsps ground cumin

1½ tsps ground coriander

1 tsp ground cardamom

½ tsp ground cinnamon

½ tsp ground nutmeg

¼ tsp ground cloves

½ tsp hot chili powder

¼ cup (55g) tomato paste (purée)

Fine sea salt

Steamed basmati rice, to serve (optional)

Small bunch of cilantro (fresh coriander), to garnish

FOR THE FRIED ONIONS

1 large onion, thinly sliced

1 tbsp all-purpose (plain) flour

½ tsp fine sea salt

1¼ cups (300ml) vegetable oil

Freshly ground black pepper

FOR THE LIME CREAM

Zest of 2 limes

⅔ cup (150ml) heavy (double) cream

SERVES 4

Loosely modeled on dal makhani, a Punjabi dal recipe made with butter and cream, this lentil dish is perfect comfort food. I use hearty chana dal here because it has bite and a structure that holds up well during cooking. To add a note of freshness, the heavy (double) cream is infused with lime zest, while the fried onions add a bit of contrasting crunch. Serve with steamed basmati rice to complete the meal.

PAIR WITH An American pale ale, or APA. With citrusy flavors that play well with the spices and enough malt to give it structure, an APA can stand up to the dal's richness and big flavors while also serving as a refreshing contrast.

THREE BEERS TO TRY Brick Brewery Peckham Pale (UK); Epic Pale Ale (NZ); Trillium Fort Point Pale Ale (US)

1 Rinse the chana dal in a sieve under cold water for a minute or two. Transfer to a large saucepan and cover with 3–4 inches (7.5–10cm) of cold water. Bring to a boil over medium-high heat, then reduce to a simmer. Cook for approximately 40 minutes or until the dal is tender, but still whole and with a bit of bite, pausing to skim off any scum that collects on the surface. Drain.

2 Meanwhile, melt the butter in a large skillet (frying pan) over medium-low heat. Once melted, add the onion and cook, stirring frequently, for 6–7 minutes, or until softened. Season with sea salt. Add the garlic, ginger, and chili pepper, and cook for 2–3 minutes, or until the raw smell has disappeared. Add all the spices and cook for another minute, or until very fragrant. Stir through the tomato paste (purée) and cook for 1–2 minutes, or until the mixture has darkened in color. Remove from the heat.

3 Return the drained chana dal to the saucepan, and add the spiced onion mixture. Top with 3 cups (750ml) water and season with a large pinch of sea salt. Increase the heat to high and bring the mixture to a boil. Once boiling, reduce the heat to medium-low and cook for another 30–35 minutes, or until the mixture has reduced and is quite thick, and the chana dal is beginning to fall apart. Stir frequently to prevent the dal sticking to the pan. If the dal looks dry at any stage, add small additions of water.

4 While the dal is cooking, make the fried onions. Add the onion, flour, sea salt, and a good amount of black pepper to a bowl, and toss gently to coat. Clean and dry your skillet, then heat the vegetable oil over high heat until hot, but not smoking. Add a slice of onion to test the heat; the oil is hot enough when it starts sizzling rapidly. Add half the onion and cook for 5–7 minutes, flipping with tongs so it cooks evenly. Once golden brown, use a slotted spoon or spider strainer to transfer the onion to a paper towel-lined plate. Repeat for the second batch. Remove the skillet from the heat and set aside.

5 Just before serving, add the lime zest to the cream and mix through to combine. Taste the dal and season with more sea salt, if necessary. If serving with basmati rice, divide the rice between the bowls. Ladle the dal on top of the rice, then drizzle with the lime cream. Top with the fried onions and cilantro (fresh coriander) and serve.

HEIRLOOM TOMATO AND WHIPPED GOAT'S CHEESE GALETTES

FOR THE GALETTE DOUGH

Scant 1 cup (105g) all-purpose (plain) flour, plus extra for dusting

½ cup (70g) rye flour

½ tsp fine sea salt

1 tsp granulated sugar

3 tbsps Parmigiano Reggiano, finely grated

1 stick (115g) unsalted butter, chilled and cubed

¼ cup (60ml) iced water

FOR THE GALETTE FILLING

1½ tbsps olive oil

1 tbsp (15g) unsalted butter

1 large onion, thinly sliced

2 medium-sized heirloom tomatoes, thinly sliced

1 egg, beaten

Flaky sea salt (such as Maldon)

FOR THE WHIPPED GOAT'S CHEESE

4½ oz (125g) soft, rindless goat's cheese

3 tbsps heavy (double) cream

½ tsp dried culinary lavender

¼ tsp fine sea salt

¼ tsp freshly ground black pepper

(Ingredients continue overleaf)

In recent years, I've grown to love galettes. Distinguished by their shaggy edges and rustic looks, these French pies can be sweet or savory, and are blessedly forgiving to make—the dough, which features rye flour and Parmigiano Reggiano, comes together in minutes in a food processor, and can be stored in the refrigerator or even frozen for future use. In the summer, a picnic-ready, heirloom-tomato galette, complemented by whipped goat's cheese, a touch of Provençal lavender, and caramelized onions, is worth turning the oven on for.

PAIR WITH A tea-infused IPA. I like what tea does to an IPA—the tannic complexity it adds, the slightly floral or even vinous character. Those notes work well against the sweetness of the tomatoes, the fragrant lavender, and the decadent goat's cheese.

THREE BEERS TO TRY Hill Farmstead Works of Love: Earl Grey Tea (US); Marble Earl Grey IPA (UK); Yeastie Boys Gunnamatta Earl Grey IPA (NZ)

1 To make the dough, add both flours, the sea salt, sugar, and Parmigiano Reggiano to a food processor, and pulse to blend. Add the butter to the flour mixture and process on low until the mixture resembles coarse meal. With the motor running, add the water in a steady stream until the dough just comes together to form a ball. If the dough looks a little dry or crumbly, add a little more water.

2 Lightly dust your hands and work surface with flour. At this stage, the dough should be relatively sticky. Scoop the dough onto the countertop and lightly dust with flour. Knead once or twice until uniform, then pat into a slightly flattened disc. Wrap with plastic wrap (clingfilm) and chill in the refrigerator for at least 30 minutes before using. (The dough can be kept in the fridge for several days, or even frozen—just defrost first.)

3 To make the filling, add the olive oil and butter to a large skillet (frying pan) and place over medium-low heat. Once the butter has just melted, add the onion and cook for approximately 30–40 minutes, stirring occasionally, until the onion is deep golden brown. If you notice the outsides of the onion beginning to scorch, reduce the heat. Once the onion is caramelized, remove from the heat and set aside.

4 Shortly before baking the galettes, preheat the oven to 400°F/200°C/Gas 6. Line a large baking sheet with parchment (baking) paper and set aside.

5 Add all the ingredients for the whipped goat's cheese to a food processor, and blend until creamy and smooth. You may need to pause and scrape down the inside of the food processor with a spatula. Set aside.

(Method continues overleaf)

Handful of cherry tomatoes

Small bunch of fresh basil leaves

Chili-infused honey, such as Mike's Hot Honey (or use regular clear honey)

Extra virgin olive oil

SERVES 4 AS A STARTER OR 2 AS A MAIN

6 Remove the dough from the fridge, and divide into two equal pieces. Set one aside. Ensure the work surface and rolling pin are well floured. Roll out the first half of dough until it's approximately ⅛-inch (3mm) thick and 9–10 inches (23–25cm) wide—you don't need a perfect round. Transfer the rolled-out dough to the baking sheet, placing it as close to one end as possible (both galettes need to fit on the baking sheet).

7 Dollop half the whipped goat's cheese in the middle of the dough round and spread out with the back of a spoon until evenly distributed, leaving a 1-inch (2.5cm) margin around the edge. Top with half the caramelized onion and heirloom tomatoes. Sprinkle the tomato slices with sea salt, to taste. Partially fold the edge of the dough over the tomatoes, leaving the middle exposed (the edge will overlap unevenly, but don't worry—that's part of the charm).

8 Roll out the second round of dough and transfer to the other side of the baking sheet. Cover with the remaining whipped goat's cheese, caramelized onion, and tomatoes (seasoning these with sea salt, to taste), and fold over the edges, as before. Brush the folded-over edge of both galettes with beaten egg using a dough (pastry) brush.

9 Bake the galettes for about 35–40 minutes, or until golden brown and the tomatoes are bubbling and beginning to darken. Let cool for 5–10 minutes.

10 Just before serving, halve the cherry tomatoes and divide between the galettes. Top with the basil leaves, followed by a drizzle of honey and extra virgin olive oil.

DINER-STYLE SMASHBURGERS

There is no better cheeseburger on Earth than the diner-style smashburger (so-called because the meat is packed into the loosest of patties before being smashed against a piping-hot skillet/frying pan with a spatula): take a bite and you can feel your dopamine receptors lighting up in real time. Smashing produces a patty with ample caramelized char and wonderfully craggy edges. The format, popularized by restaurants such as In-N-Out and Shake Shack, also demands other additions: a tangy burger sauce, melting American cheese, piquant pickles, plus onions (here, both raw and caramelized). The result is simply so much more satisfying than any other burger out there.

PAIR WITH A hazy pale ale or IPA. A burger that serves up as much richness, acidic tang (the burger sauce and pickles), and sweetness (the caramelized onions) needs a beer that can stand up to it. A hazy IPA both matches its intensity and tempers all that beef and dribbling cheese.

THREE BEERS TO TRY DEYA Steady Rolling Man (UK); Garage Beer Soup (Spain); The Alchemist Heady Topper (US)

1lb (450g) 20%-fat ground (minced) beef

4 burger buns (preferably Martin's Potato Rolls)

1 tbsp olive oil

4 slices American cheese

½ sweet onion, sliced into thin rings

Sliced pickles

Ketchup (optional)

Yellow mustard (optional)

Flaky sea salt (such as Maldon) and freshly ground black pepper

FOR THE BURGER SAUCE

3 tbsps mayonnaise

1 tbsp sriracha mayonnaise (or use ½ tbsp sriracha and ½ tbsp regular mayonnaise)

1½ tbsps ketchup

1 tbsp yellow mustard

1 tsp pickle brine

FOR THE CARAMELIZED ONIONS

3 tbsps (45g) unsalted butter

2 tsps olive oil

2 medium sweet onions, finely diced

SERVES 4

1 Begin by making the caramelized onions. Heat the butter and olive oil in a large skillet (frying pan) over medium-low heat. Once the butter has melted, reduce the heat to low and add the onions. Cook, stirring occasionally, for approximately 30–40 minutes, or until the onions turn deep golden brown. Ensure the heat is low enough to avoid scorching the onions. Remove the onions from the skillet and set aside.

2 Meanwhile, to prepare the burger patties, remove the beef from the refrigerator 45 minutes to 1 hour before cooking to bring it to room temperature. Divide the beef into four equal portions, but don't pack the meat down into a tight puck. Instead, loosely shape each portion into a tennis ball-sized sphere that only just holds together. Season each sphere with a pinch of sea salt and black pepper, then gently rotate and season on the other side. Set aside.

3 To make the burger sauce, mix all the ingredients together in a small bowl or ramekin, and set aside.

4 Once the onions are caramelized and the meat at room temperature, you're ready to cook the burgers. Place a large, heavy-bottomed skillet (frying pan)—preferably made from cast iron—over medium-low heat. Slice the buns in half and place both halves, cut-sides down, in the skillet (you will probably need to do this in two batches). Toast the buns for 3–5 minutes or until golden brown. Once all the buns are toasted, remove the skillet from the heat and carefully wipe out any crumbs.

5 Divide the buns between four plates. Add a large dollop of burger sauce to the bottom half of each bun, spreading to the edges with the back of a spoon, followed by a quarter of the caramelized onions.

6 Return the skillet to the stovetop, increase the heat to high, and add the olive oil. Once the oil is very hot, but not smoking, add two of the patties and smash them down with a spatula until they are about ½-inch (1cm) thick. Each patty should be quite wide, with loose, craggy edges. Cook for about 2 minutes, or until the patties develop a nice, caramelized char. Flip and place a slice of American cheese on each. Cook for a further 1½ minutes or so, or until the underside of each patty is charred and the cheese has melted. Transfer to the prepared buns and repeat for the remaining two patties.

7 Top each burger with several rings of sweet onion, pickle slices, and more burger sauce or small dollops of ketchup and mustard, as preferred. Serve immediately.

JERK JACKFRUIT WITH COCONUT RICE AND PINEAPPLE SALSA

4 scallions (spring onions), both white and green parts, roughly chopped

Thumb-sized piece of fresh ginger, peeled and roughly chopped

4 large garlic cloves, roughly chopped

1 tbsp fresh thyme leaves

2 tbsps soy sauce

2 tbsps vegetable oil, divided

½ tsp ground allspice

½ tsp ground cinnamon

¼ tsp ground cloves

½ tsp fine sea salt

1 tsp Scotch bonnet-based hot sauce (or more, depending on how hot your sauce is)

Juice of 1 lime

1 large onion, thinly sliced

9oz (250g) fresh jackfruit segments

1⅔ cups (400ml) vegetable stock

1 tbsp dark brown sugar

1 tbsp tomato paste (purée)

Freshly ground black pepper

FOR THE COCONUT RICE

1 cup (170g) basmati rice

1 tbsp vegetable oil

½ onion, finely diced

1 garlic clove, finely chopped

(Ingredients continue overleaf)

Jackfruit is a pretty miraculous thing. Sweet and lightly pungent when eaten raw, it takes on a texture reminiscent of pulled pork when stewed and then roasted. That quality has made it a favorite of vegans in the last few years, but avowed carnivores can certainly enjoy it, too—especially when it's cooked down with a spicy jerk marinade and served alongside coconut rice. Note that while young jackfruit (typically sold in cans) is frequently called for in recipes, skip that here: the balance of seasoning is tailored to the sweetness of the fresh fruit.

PAIR WITH A tropical IPA. Many IPAs are described as having tropical-fruit flavor profiles, from pineapple and mango to passion fruit and papaya. Choose a fruit-led IPA, then, to pick up the natural sweetness of the jackfruit and the pineapple salsa.

THREE BEERS TO TRY Lervig Tasty Juice (Norway); Northern Monk Mango Lassi Heathen (UK); Tree House Green (US)

1 To make the jerk-spice paste, add the scallions (spring onions), ginger, garlic, thyme, soy sauce, 1 tablespoon of the vegetable oil, the spices, sea salt, hot sauce, lime juice, and black pepper (to taste) to a food processor or blender. Blend on high for 2–3 minutes, or until you have a thick, uniform paste. Pause to scrape down the inside of the food processor/blender with a spatula, if necessary.

2 Add the remaining tablespoon of vegetable oil to a large saucepan, and place over medium heat. Once the oil is hot, add the onion and cook, stirring frequently, for 7–8 minutes, or until softened. Add the jerk-spice paste and cook for a further minute. Stir in the jackfruit and vegetable stock. Increase the heat to medium-high and bring the mixture to a boil. Once boiling, reduce to a simmer and cover. Cook, stirring occasionally, for approximately 45 minutes, or until the jackfruit has softened and is beginning to break down.

3 Remove the lid from the pan—if the jackfruit segments are still relatively whole, use a fork to separate them into smaller pieces. Stir in the sugar and tomato paste (purée). If the mixture is still slightly watery, increase the heat to medium-high and, stirring frequently, cook for a further 5–10 minutes, or until it is thick and stew-like. Remove from the heat.

4 Preheat the oven to 350°F/180°C/Gas 4. Line a large baking sheet with nonstick foil. Spread the jackfruit mixture over the foil in a thin, single layer. Bake for about 30–35 minutes—removing the sheet halfway through to stir the mixture and rotate the sheet—or until it is darkened around the edges, thickened, and has the consistency of pulled pork. Use a fork to shred the pieces further, if you wish.

(Method continues overleaf)

¾ cup plus 2 tbsps (205ml) coconut milk

⅔ cup (150ml) water

2 sprigs fresh thyme

1 tsp fine sea salt

FOR THE PINEAPPLE SALSA

10½ oz (300g) fresh pineapple flesh, cut into small cubes

Juice of 1 lime

1 scallion (spring onion), thinly sliced

Small bunch of cilantro (fresh coriander)

Large pinch of flaky sea salt (such as Maldon)

Freshly ground black pepper

SERVES 2

5 Meanwhile, to cook the coconut rice, rinse the rice in a sieve under cold water for several minutes, or until the water runs clear. Set aside.

6 Heat the vegetable oil in a small saucepan over medium heat. Once the oil is hot, add the onion and cook for 2–3 minutes. Add the garlic and cook for a further minute. Next, add the rice, coconut milk, water, thyme sprigs, and sea salt, and increase the heat to high. Once the mixture begins to boil, cover, reduce the heat to medium-low, and cook for 10 minutes. Remove the pan from the heat, keeping the lid on, and allow the rice to steam for a further 10 minutes. Once the rice is cooked, fluff lightly with a fork and remove the thyme sprigs.

7 Just before serving, make the pineapple salsa by adding all the ingredients to a bowl and tossing lightly to combine.

8 Divide the coconut rice between the plates and top with the shredded jackfruit. Serve with the pineapple salsa on the side.

FUSILLI WITH CHANTERELLE CREAM SAUCE

1lb (450g) chanterelle or girolle mushrooms

3 tbsps olive oil

2 tbsps (30g) unsalted butter, divided

1 large onion, finely diced

4 garlic cloves, finely chopped

¼ cup (60ml) Amontillado sherry or white wine

1 cup (250ml) heavy (double) cream

½ tsp nutmeg (preferably freshly grated)

1lb (450g) fusilli

About ½ cup (45g) shaved Parmigiano Reggiano, plus extra to serve

Small bunch of fresh tarragon leaves, roughly chopped

Fine sea salt and freshly ground black pepper

SERVES 4 TO 5

Golden, glorious chanterelles, known for their peppery—even fruity—flavor, are prized during their summer growing season. With mushrooms this special, it's best to treat them simply, and a classic cream sauce is just the ticket. Add a dusting of nutmeg and also a splash of Amontillado sherry, if you can find it (its nutty salinity was made for mushrooms). While you can serve this sauce with any number of pasta shapes (pappardelle is a typical candidate), I like the way it hugs and coats each twist of fusilli. Finish with a small handful of fresh tarragon, which adds a bit of levity and freshness.

PAIR WITH A malty, West Coast-style IPA. Perhaps surprisingly, the caramel sweetness of malt-driven IPAs tends to pair seamlessly with umami flavors (in this case, the mushrooms and Parmigiano Reggiano).

THREE BEERS TO TRY Alpine Duet (US); Buxton Axe Edge IPA (UK); Odell IPA (US)

1 First, clean the mushrooms. Use a mushroom brush (or toothbrush) to remove any dirt and grit from each mushroom. Don't wash the mushrooms with water, as that will make them swell and soften. Tear into rough pieces and set aside.

2 Heat the olive oil and half the butter in a large skillet (frying pan) over medium-high heat. Once the butter has melted, add the onion and cook for 6–7 minutes, or until softened and translucent. Season to taste with sea salt and black pepper (a pinch of each should be enough). Add the garlic and cook for a further 1–2 minutes. Add the mushrooms and cook for another 5–6 minutes, or until tender.

3 Pour in the Amontillado sherry or wine and stir well, cooking for several minutes until it has largely evaporated. Reduce the heat to low, add the cream, and cook for several minutes at a low simmer. Season with the nutmeg and sea salt and black pepper, to taste. Remove from the heat.

4 Meanwhile, cook the fusilli in boiling salted water in a medium saucepan, according to the directions on the packet or until al dente. Drain the fusilli, reserving about 1 cup (250ml) of the cooking water.

5 Toss the fusilli in the skillet until coated with the cream mixture. Add the remaining butter, the Parmigiano Reggiano, and a good slosh of the pasta water—you probably won't use all of it—and stir well. The sauce should be glossy and uniform, and coat the pasta evenly; add slightly more pasta water if it looks as if it needs more moisture.

6 Divide the fusilli between bowls and top with the fresh tarragon and extra Parmigiano Reggiano, to taste. Serve immediately.

INDIAN-SPICED FRIED CHICKEN

FOR THE SPICE MIX

3 tbsps garam masala

3 tsps ground cumin

2 tsps ground coriander

1 tsp ground turmeric

1½ tsps chili powder

FOR THE BRINE

1½ cups (390g) Greek yogurt

6 garlic cloves, crushed

Thumb-sized piece of fresh ginger, peeled and roughly chopped

2 bird's-eye chili peppers, finely chopped

Scant 1 cup (190ml) whole milk

2 tsps fine sea salt

FOR THE FRIED CHICKEN

2lb (900g) bone-in, skin-on chicken thighs and drumsticks

About 8 cups (2 liters) vegetable oil

2 cups (300g) 00-grade pasta flour

1 tsp fine sea salt

Flaky sea salt (such as Maldon)

1 scallion (spring onion), thinly sliced, and cilantro (fresh coriander) leaves, to garnish (optional)

SERVES 4

For a relatively simple dish, fried chicken is enormously contentious: every recipe seems to promise a different technique for nailing that prized combination of crisper-than-crisp exterior and juicy meat. I don't purport to have the ultimate formula, but I do think this recipe delivers the goods. In lieu of the traditional buttermilk, I like to marinate my chicken overnight in a spiced, yogurt-based brine, almost as if I were making tikka masala. For a crispy coating that's full of nooks and crannies, I skip the cornstarch (cornflour) and double-dredging, and instead use a tip learned from Serious Eats: go for 00-grade flour (an extra-fine flour normally used for pasta), which makes for a light and shatteringly crisp coating. Finishing each piece with a dusting of spices gives this fried chicken extra pep.

PAIR WITH A session IPA: with its complex hop profile, but light body, a session IPA serves up big flavors and refreshment simultaneously. Alternatively, try a Belgian pale ale, or BPA. Light and sessionable, but with a classic, ester-driven flavor profile thanks to the Belgian yeast, BPAs are as food-friendly as it gets.

THREE BEERS TO TRY Brasserie de la Senne Taras Boulba (Belgium); Brasserie d'Orval Orval (Belgium); Lawson's Finest Liquids Super Session #2 (US)

1 You need to brine the chicken for 8–12 hours before frying, so begin preparations on the morning you plan to cook. First, make the spice mix by adding all the spices to a small bowl and mixing until uniform. Set aside.

2 To prepare the brine, add the yogurt, garlic, ginger, chili peppers, and one-third of the spice mix to a large bowl. Stir well to mix. Slowly pour in the milk, stirring as you go, until the brining mixture has the consistency of cream. Season with the sea salt and stir to combine.

3 Place the chicken thighs and drumsticks in the brine, and submerge as much as possible. Cover and chill in the refrigerator for 8–12 hours.

4 Remove the bowl from the refrigerator about 45 minutes before frying the chicken and let come to room temperature. Leave the chicken in the brining mixture.

5 Add the vegetable oil to a large Dutch oven (or large, flameproof casserole dish), preferably made from cast iron. The oil should come roughly halfway up the pot; add more if your pot is especially large. Clip a deep-fat-frying thermometer to the inside of the pot and increase the heat to high. Wait until the oil reaches a temperature of 325°F (160°C)—this will take about 10–15 minutes, depending on your stove.

(Method continues overleaf)

6 While the oil is heating up, organize your frying station. Line a large baking sheet with paper towels and place a wire rack on top; this is where the chicken will rest after frying. Mix the flour, fine sea salt, and another third of the spice mix in a large bowl. Use a spoon to drizzle approximately 3 tablespoons of the brining liquid over the flour and toss gently to combine—this adds extra pieces that will adhere to the chicken and make it even craggier and crisper.

7 Once the oil has just reached the required temperature, take the first piece of chicken from the brining liquid and let any excess drip off. Transfer the chicken to the bowl and cover with the flour mixture, ensuring it is thoroughly and evenly coated. Gently shake off any excess flour, then drop the chicken into the oil (be careful, as the oil will bubble up fiercely). Repeat the battering process immediately with several other pieces of chicken, so 3–4 pieces cook simultaneously. (Depending on the size of the pot, you will probably have to cook the chicken in 2–3 batches.)

8 The oil temperature will fall to around 300°F (150°C) or slightly lower when you add the chicken before rising slowly as it cooks. Use tongs to gently rotate the chicken, to ensure it browns evenly.

9 After 10 minutes, begin checking the internal temperature of the chicken every couple of minutes by removing a piece with tongs and inserting a meat thermometer in the thickest part. Be careful not to touch the bone—the chicken is properly cooked when it reaches 165°F (74°C). If necessary, cook for a further 5–6 minutes, checking the temperature regularly as before. Please note: cooking times will vary depending on the size of the chicken pieces.

10 Transfer the cooked chicken to the prepared baking sheet. Season both sides lightly with flaky sea salt and some of the remaining spice mix. Garnish with the sliced scallions (spring onions) and cilantro (coriander) leaves, if using. Repeat the deep-frying and seasoning process for the remaining batches of chicken. Ensure the fried chicken is cool enough to handle before serving.

BEER AND CHILIS BY JEN FERGUSON

Chilis are the second part of the Hop Burns & Black holy trinity. We've made hot sauces with beer in them and beers with chilis in them. We're all about the heat.

Chili peppers come in a range of strengths, from mild to super-hot, and as new varieties are developed all the time, super-hot just keeps on getting hotter. Though we stock a few scorchingly spicy sauces, these are typically sold for novelty value (and to cater to Secret Santa shoppers looking to prank their co-workers).

We much prefer sauces that combine heat and flavor, and which really bring out the unique characteristics of the chilis they use—the fruitiness of a Scotch bonnet, the smokiness of a chipotle, the earthiness of a poblano...

There are a few pointers to keep in mind when pairing beer and chili-infused dishes. If you're cooking with an especially spicy sauce or chili pepper, you might want to avoid that can of pale ale or IPA: rather than cooling capsaicin, bitterness heightens the heat. Instead, look for a more malt-driven style to temper the flames. Schwarzbiers and amber ales are both good alternatives, and dish out plenty of refreshment alongside stir-frys, noodle dishes, or jerk chicken.

If you're making a super-flavorful, intensely spiced dish—carne adovada, say, or slow-cooked pulled pork—turn to a brown ale, dunkelweizen, porter, or stout. These styles feature strong malt profiles that stand up to bold flavors while also providing a cooling effect. Smoky dark styles, like German rauchbiers or smoked porters, are great to accompany or evoke flame-cooked barbecue fare.

If you want to keep the spice in check, be wary of beers with very high ABVs, as alcohol can also emphasize chili heat. Save the imperial beers for another meal—unless, of course, you want to turn the heat up to 11!

JEN'S MICHELADA-MARY-MASH-UP

½ cup (125ml) tomato or Clamato juice

1 tbsp Worcestershire sauce

½ tsp balsamic vinegar

½ tsp soy sauce

1 tsp hot sauce of your choice (more if you like it spicy)

Pinch of cayenne pepper

2 limes

Coarse salt, for a decorative rim

1 16fl oz (475ml) can citrusy gose

Fine sea salt and freshly ground black pepper, to taste

Ice, to serve

MAKES 2

This is one of my go-to, slap-up weekend drinks—the ultimate hangover cure or simply a general restorative. An unholy mash-up of a bloody Mary and a michelada, it was inspired by an amazing lunch at Mexican restaurant Cosme in New York in 2016, where we enjoyed a michelada (or two) made with Two Roads x Evil Twin's Geyser Gose. It was so delicious that we still talk about it to this day—along with the fact that Barack and Michelle Obama had eaten there the day before. I bet they had the michelada...

The joy here is that you don't need to be precise—make it to your taste, increase and decrease quantities as you like, and throw it together. Just don't skimp on the limes!

1 Whisk together the tomato juice, Worcestershire sauce, balsamic vinegar, soy sauce, hot sauce, and cayenne pepper in a small pitcher (jug).

2 Juice one of the limes, add to the tomato mixture, and stir through. Season to taste with sea salt and black pepper.

3 Cut the other lime into four wedges. Pour several tablespoons of coarse salt onto a saucer or small plate. Rub the rim of the glasses with a lime wedge, then dip the rim in the salt to coat.

4 Fill the glasses with ice and split the tomato juice mixture equally between them. Top with the gose, stir gently to combine, and garnish each glass with a lime wedge.

SHRIMP AND MANGO COCONUT CURRY

FOR THE CURRY PASTE

5–6 garlic cloves, chopped

Thumb-sized piece of fresh ginger, peeled and roughly chopped

2 bird's-eye chili peppers, roughly chopped

Small bunch of cilantro (fresh coriander) stems, roughly chopped

Juice of 1 lime

Large pinch of flaky sea salt (such as Maldon)

FOR THE CURRY

2–3 tbsps vegetable oil or ghee

1 onion, thinly sliced

20 curry leaves, divided

1½ tsps ground coriander

1 tsp ground turmeric

¼ tsp asafetida

2–3 tbsps tomato paste (purée)

1 14fl oz (400ml) can coconut milk

7 tbsps (105ml) water

1 ripe mango, peeled, pitted (stoned), and cut into matchsticks, divided (reserve a few to garnish)

7oz (200g) large shrimp (jumbo prawns), ideally heads-on and unpeeled

Fine sea salt and freshly cracked black pepper

Cilantro (fresh coriander) leaves, roughly chopped, and 1 red chili, sliced (optional), to garnish

Steamed basmati rice, to serve

SERVES 4

Double IPAs are one of my favorite beer styles, but their high alcohol levels and intense flavor profiles can make them tricky to pair with food. When looking for a perfect pairing, I reverse-engineered this South Indian-style curry recipe. It supplies richness and sweetness in the form of a coconut-milk base and uses fresh mango to evoke tropical-fruit flavors. The full-on hop pungency of a classic DIPA is matched by what I think of as the curry's pivotal ingredient: asafetida. The merest amount of this powerful spice is enough to transform the dish and add a beguiling, savory edge.

PAIR WITH A hazy double IPA. Though Double IPAs are a notoriously tricky style to pair, this curry stands up to the task with its own bold flavors and tropical appeal.

THREE BEERS TO TRY Foundation Brewing Co Epiphany (US); Liberty Brewing C!tra Double IPA (NZ); Verdant Pulp Double IPA (UK)

1 To prepare the curry paste, blend all the ingredients in a food processor on high speed until well mixed, pausing to scrape down the insides. Set aside.

2 To make the curry, heat the vegetable oil/ghee in a large, heavy-bottomed skillet (frying pan) over medium-high heat. Once the oil/ghee is hot, add the onion and cook, stirring frequently, for 7–8 minutes, or until softened and translucent. Add the curry paste and fry for a further 2–3 minutes, stirring frequently. Add 10 of the curry leaves and fry for a further minute. Add the coriander, turmeric, and asafetida, and fry for a further 30 seconds before adding the tomato paste (purée). Cook for 1–2 minutes more, stirring constantly.

3 Add the coconut milk and water to the skillet and stir to combine. Season generously with sea salt. Add half the mango pieces, reduce the heat to medium-low, then let simmer and gradually reduce for 25–30 minutes. The sauce should thicken and turn a rich, dark orange hue. Season to taste.

4 Shortly before serving, add the remaining curry leaves, mango pieces, and shrimp (prawns). Depending on the size of the skillet, you may need to cook the shrimp in two batches. Press the shrimp into the curry until covered by as much liquid as possible and cook for roughly 1½ minutes, or until pink on one side. Flip and let cook for a further 1–1½ minutes. Note: I prefer to use whole shrimp, but you can also use the peeled and deveined variety, if you prefer. If so, cook for a maximum of 45 seconds to 1 minute per side.

5 Once the shrimp are cooked through, remove the curry from the heat, garnish with the cilantro (fresh coriander) leaves, sliced chili (optional), and reserved mango matchsticks, then serve with steamed basmati rice.

STEAK WITH FOIE GRAS AND ONION SAUCE

2 sirloin steaks, about 10oz (285g) each

2 small, ½-inch (1cm) thick slices foie gras (optional)

1 tbsp olive oil, plus a little extra for the foie gras

Flaky sea salt (such as Maldon) and freshly ground black pepper

FOR THE ONION SAUCE

1 large onion

3 tbsps (45g) unsalted butter, divided

1½ tbsps sherry vinegar

5 tbsps (75ml) chicken stock

5 tbsps (75ml) Madeira

Large pinch of granulated sugar

Flaky sea salt and freshly ground black pepper

SERVES 2

I'll admit it—this dish is borderline absurd. It feels opulent and ostentatious, food fit for a king. The onion sauce has some acidity, but this is mostly richness, and fat, piled up in multiple layers. But there are times when excess is just right, and that's when this recipe should be called on. It is even better once you're two beers deep.

PAIR WITH A bold IPA or double IPA. A dish of this richness needs something powerful to temper it, and a big, bitter, hop-driven IPA or DIPA is exactly what's needed.

THREE BEERS TO TRY Bissell Brothers Swish (US); Kaiju! Aftermath (Australia); Magic Rock Cannonball IPA (UK)

1 Preferably the night before cooking, but at least 5 hours before, season both sides of the steaks with plenty of sea salt and pepper. Cover and chill in the refrigerator (this tenderizes the proteins in the meat). Remove the steaks from the fridge 1 hour before cooking, along with the foie gras slices (if using), and let come to room temperature.

2 Before cooking the steaks, begin the onion sauce by peeling and halving the onion, then slice each half into ½-inch (1cm) wide strips, cutting across the width of the onion rather than end-to-end. Separate the slices into individual layers and set aside.

3 If using foie gras, lightly score both sides of each slice and season with a small pinch of sea salt and black pepper. Note that foie gras terrine won't work here.

4 To cook the steaks, heat the olive oil in a large, heavy-bottomed skillet (frying pan) over high heat. Once the oil is very hot, add both steaks and cook for 2 minutes on the first side without disturbing, to allow a nice caramelized crust to form. Flip the steaks over and cook on the other side for approximately 1½ minutes for medium-rare (increase the cooking time slightly if you prefer your steak more well done). If the steak has a band of fat around the edge, use tongs to sear this directly against the skillet. Transfer the steaks to two serving plates and let rest for 10 minutes.

5 Finish making the onion sauce while the steaks are resting. With the heat still on high, add 1 tablespoon (15g) of the butter and the sliced onion to the skillet. Fry for 2–3 minutes, or until the onion slices are softened and beginning to turn golden.

6 Deglaze the skillet with the sherry vinegar and stir, using a spoon to scrape up any tasty brown bits that have accumulated on the bottom of the skillet.

7 Add the chicken stock, Madeira, sugar, a small pinch of sea salt, and lots of black pepper. Cook for 1–2 minutes. After the sauce has partially reduced, add the remaining 2 tablespoons (30g) of butter and stir. Reduce for a further 1–2 minutes until the sauce begins to thicken. Remove from the heat, and divide the sauce between the steaks.

8 If using foie gras, rinse and wipe out the skillet, return to a high heat, and add a drop of olive oil. Once the oil is very hot, add the foie gras and cook for 30 seconds on each side or until they begin to brown. Top each steak with a slice of foie gras and serve.

PAN-FRIED LAMB CHOPS WITH RAMPS PESTO

6 lamb rib or loin chops

1–2 tbsps olive oil

Flaky sea salt (such as Maldon) and freshly ground black pepper

FOR THE RAMPS PESTO

Large bunch of ramps (wild garlic) (about 1½ oz/40g)

3 tbsps extra virgin olive oil

Zest and juice of 1 lemon

1 tsp granulated sugar

1 tsp flaky sea salt

Freshly ground black pepper

SERVES 2

Spring is the perfect time to make this dish. Ramps—often known as wild garlic or ramsons—are in season for only a brief window each year, but their fresh, pungent flavor makes them a favorite of both chefs and amateur foragers. If you manage to get your hands on any ramps, use as the base for a potent pesto and serve alongside gamy lamb chops. While it's wise to get started early and salt your lamb overnight, once prepped, this dish takes just minutes to cook up.

PAIR WITH An oniony IPA or pale ale. Some tasters note that hops like Mosaic and Citra can have a savory, even allium-like flavor. That dose of pungency works beautifully alongside the ramps pesto.

THREE BEERS TO TRY Brouwerij Kees Mosaic Hop Explosion (Netherlands); Cloudwater IPA Citra (UK); Thomas Hooker Brewery #NOFILTER IPA (US)

1 The night before cooking the lamb—or at least several hours before—season both sides of the chops with sea salt and black pepper, to taste. Place in the refrigerator in a Ziploc bag or covered container, to help tenderize the proteins in the meat.

2 Remove the lamb from the refrigerator about an hour before cooking and let come to room temperature.

3 Meanwhile, to make the pesto, blend all the ingredients in a food processor. If necessary, pause and scrape down the insides of the food processor with a spatula to ensure all the leafy bits are evenly incorporated. Taste and adjust the seasoning, if required. Set aside.

4 Add the olive oil to a heavy-bottomed skillet (frying pan), preferably made from cast iron, and place over high heat. Once the oil is hot, but not smoking, cook the chops on one side for 1½–2 minutes, or until they have a nice brown crust. (If using loin chops, cook for 2½–3 minutes.) Flip the chops over and cook for a further 1–1½ minutes (or 2–2½ minutes for loin chops), depending on how well done you like your lamb. Remove from the heat, transfer to plates, and let rest for 10 minutes.

5 Just before serving, drizzle the chops with the ramps pesto. (You may not use all the pesto, but it will keep in an airtight container in the refrigerator for a few days.)

PEACH UPSIDE-DOWN CAKE WITH MISO CARAMEL

1 stick (115g) unsalted butter, softened, plus extra for greasing

3 ripe peaches, halved, pitted (stoned), and cut into ¼-inch (5mm) pieces

Heaping 1 cup (130g) all-purpose (plain) flour

1 tsp baking powder

1 tsp ground cardamom

¾ cup (150g) granulated sugar

3 eggs, at room temperature

FOR THE MISO CARAMEL

¼ cup (60ml) water

¾ cup (150g) granulated sugar

½ cup (125ml) heavy (double) cream, at room temperature

1½ tbsps white miso paste

SERVES 10 TO 12

I first came across a recipe for miso caramel on the Food52 website, and have made it a staple of my desserts ever since: it's wonderful in an apple crumble and even better on vanilla ice cream. As someone who's always loved salted caramel—or any dessert with a savory element—miso caramel is a flavor-packed winner. Recently, I've particularly enjoyed it in this peach upside-down cake. As in a tarte tatin, the fruit cooks in the caramel; when the cake is fully baked and flipped, a deep, burnished layer of caramel-doused peaches is revealed.

PAIR WITH A West Coast-style IPA. Carrot cake and IPA is a classic pairing, and I like the way this cake works with the style, too. Opt for an IPA with a caramel malt profile, which also complements the umami of the miso caramel.

THREE BEERS TO TRY 8 Wired HopWired IPA (NZ); Ithaca Beer Company Flower Power (US); Siren Craft Brew Soundwave (UK)

1 First, prepare the miso caramel. Add the water and sugar to a heavy-bottomed saucepan, stir briefly to combine, then place over high heat. Once the sugar has completely dissolved and the mixture is starting to bubble, resist stirring (although you can swirl the pan gently or use a wet dough (pastry) brush to incorporate any errant sugar crystals on the sides of the pan).

2 Let the mixture boil for approximately 8–10 minutes, or until it darkens to a deep amber—once the mixture begins changing color, watch carefully as it will caramelize quickly. Remove from the heat once the mixture has turned dark amber, then immediately add the cream in a slow, steady stream, whisking rapidly to incorporate. The mixture will bubble up when the cream is first added, so use caution.

3 Once the cream is fully incorporated and the caramel is smooth, return the pan to a low heat, add the miso paste, and whisk until smooth. Remove from the heat and set aside.

4 Preheat the oven to 350°F/180°C/Gas 4. Grease a 9-inch (23cm) cake pan (tin), preferably springform, with butter and line the bottom with parchment (baking) paper (grease this as well). Starting at the center of the pan, arrange the peach pieces in a spiral pattern, overlapping them as you go, until they cover the base of the whole pan. Pour over half the caramel mixture and set aside.

5 Sift the flour, baking powder, and cardamom into a medium bowl. Set aside. In another medium bowl, cream together the softened butter and sugar for 4–5 minutes, or until light yellow and very fluffy. Beat the eggs into the butter/sugar mixture, one at a time, until fully incorporated, pausing to scrape down the sides of the bowl. Add the flour mixture and beat in gently until just combined.

6 Pour the cake batter over the peaches and spread out carefully to the edges of the pan, being careful not to disturb the peach layer. Place the pan on a baking tray and transfer to the oven. Bake for 35–45 minutes, or until the cake has risen, is nicely golden, and a skewer inserted part-way through (avoiding the peach layer) comes out clean.

7 Remove the cake pan from the oven and let cool on a cooling rack for 5–10 minutes. If using a springform pan, release and remove the sides; if not, use a knife to gently separate the cake from the sides of the pan. Place a large serving plate over the pan and gently flip so that the cake is upside-down. Carefully remove the base of the pan and baking paper, and return any dislodged peach slices.

8 Pour the remaining miso caramel over the cake, and serve.

PISTACHIO SAFFRON CUPCAKES

1 cup plus 2 tbsps (150g) shelled raw pistachios

1⅛ cups (150g) all-purpose (plain) flour

Heaping 1 cup (225g) superfine (caster) sugar

1½ tsps baking powder

¾ tsp fine sea salt

1 cup (250ml) boiling water

Large pinch of saffron strands

2 tsps vanilla paste or vanilla extract

½ cup (125ml) vegetable oil

2 eggs, at room temperature

Zest of 1 orange

FOR THE FROSTING AND TOPPING

½ cup (100g) mascarpone

½ cup (85g) pistachio cream or butter (available from specialist Italian food stores)

2 tsps whole milk

1–2 tbsps powdered (icing) sugar (optional)

3 tbsps shelled raw pistachios

Orange zest, to garnish

MAKES ABOUT 16 CUPCAKES

Sure, a cupcake is pretty passé: childish, even. But these cupcakes feel appealingly adult—perhaps it's the fact that there's not a sprinkle in sight. With ground pistachios in the batter, a frosting made of pistachio butter, and toasted pistachios on top, they're nutty and vividly green, while the saffron adds a perfumed complexity. If you can, look for sweet Sicilian pistachio cream (such as Pariani) to add to the frosting. If you can't find it, pistachio nut butter works in a pinch, along with some extra sugar.

PAIR WITH A malt-driven pale ale or IPA. Choose one made with crystal malt or with its own dose of sweetness, and steer away from anything too bracing or astringent.

THREE BEERS TO TRY Sierra Nevada Pale Ale (US); Tröegs Perpetual IPA (US); Wylam Brewery Jakehead IPA (UK)

1 Preheat the oven to 350°F/180°C/Gas 4. Line a cupcake pan (tray) with cupcake wrappers (or grease with butter and lightly flour).

2 To make the cupcake batter, finely grind the pistachios in a food processor and add to a bowl, along with the flour, sugar, baking powder, and sea salt. Mix to combine.

3 Add the boiling water to a bowl with the saffron strands and infuse for 5–10 minutes.

4 Add the vanilla paste/extract and vegetable oil to a medium bowl. Pour in the saffron water, strands and all, and stir to combine. Create a well in the center of the dry ingredients and slowly whisk in the liquid ingredients.

5 Lightly whisk the eggs in a small bowl, add to the cake batter along with the orange zest, and whisk again to combine. The batter will be quite thin, so transfer to a liquid measuring cup or pitcher (jug) to make it easier to fill the cupcake wrappers.

6 Carefully fill each wrapper to the top with the cake batter. Bake for 20–25 minutes, rotating halfway through, or until the cupcakes have risen, are golden brown on top, and a toothpick comes out quite (but not entirely) clean. Remove from the oven and let cool in the pan for 5 minutes before transferring to a cooling rack.

7 Meanwhile, to prepare the frosting (icing), combine the mascarpone, pistachio cream/butter, and milk in a small bowl. The frosting should be glossy, thick, and spreadable. Add a tiny bit more milk if the frosting is still quite thick. Depending on the variety of pistachio cream, you may also wish to sweeten the frosting with 1–2 tablespoons of powdered (icing) sugar.

8 Toast the pistachios in a small skillet (frying pan) over medium-high heat, tossing frequently, for approximately 5–6 minutes, or until the pistachios start to brown and smell fragrant. Remove from the heat and set aside.

9 Once cool, dollop each cupcake with frosting and swirl with a knife to cover. Top each cupcake with a few toasted pistachios and a pinch of orange zest. The cupcakes will keep in an airtight container in the refrigerator for up to 4–5 days.

CHAPTER 5 | DARK BEERS

GUIDE TO DARK BEER STYLES BY JEN FERGUSON

Black butter vanilla volcano salt mocha white chocolate ganache. That's not a random word salad, it's an actual beer description. The beer in question? Amurga, an imperial stout brewed by the Swedish brewery Omnipollo.

Dark beer as a category is so vast that it's hard to make any generalizations about it. It covers an enormous variety of styles, made in very different ways and across a huge spectrum of flavors. Dark beers can range from the sublimely understated to the borderline ridiculous; from classic German altbiers to roasty London porters to baroque "pastry stouts" like the above. As a wise man (Evin O'Riordain, founder of The Kernel Brewery—you can read more about him later in this introduction) once said, "There is nothing inherent about 'dark beers' other than their color, and that is covered in the name already."

Amid the sheer multitude of dark styles, we've covered a few in other places (read more about dark sours, schwarzbiers, dark wheat beers, and black IPAs in previous chapters). Here, however, is a guide to the other major dark styles you shouldn't miss.

BROWN ALES AND ALTBIERS

Woefully underrated, untrendy brown ale deserves far more credit than it gets. It's a beautiful style, perfect for when you crave malty character without the over-the-top punch of a stout (though imperial versions do exist). Brown ales are usually sweet and malty, with nutty or caramel notes, though English styles tend to be sweeter than American styles, which often up the hop content. Derived from the traditional English mild, a style named more for its lack of hop bitterness than its alcohol content, brown ales work as an excellent foil to spicy dishes, as their lack of bitterness helps temper the heat.

Like brown ales, altbiers ("old beers") also merit more attention than they receive. Originally from Düsseldorf, altbiers are made with top-fermenting ale yeast but, like lagers, are conditioned at cold temperatures for long periods. The result is a malt-forward style that is still wonderfully clean, with a peppery hop snap to complement the nutty, toasty aromas. The style's balance between malt and hops makes it a versatile pairing partner.

SMOKED BEERS AND SPICED BEERS

The most famous smoked beers in the world are brewed by Schlenkerla in Bamberg, Bavaria. Rauchbiers—literally meaning "smoke beers"—are Schlenkerla's specialty, and have a distinct flavor thanks to the malts, which are roasted according to traditional methods over beechwood fires. The most popular of Schlenkerla's rauchbiers is the dark amber Märzen (or "bacon beer," as we like to call it). Boisterously smoky on the nose and palate, this beer is an obvious match for German sausages and other hearty fare, but bizarrely it also works well with feisty mint chocolate.

Of course, you don't need to be in Bavaria to make a smoked beer. Any beer using smoked malt will have pleasingly kindled characteristics. We even made one ourselves: Aztec Challenge Smoked Porter, a collaboration with Elusive Brewing. (Of course, being Hop Burns & Black, we couldn't resist putting chili in it.)

Speaking of unusual ingredients: spiced beers are another iteration of dark beer that involve surprising flavors. Pumpkin beer, for years a phenomenally popular style across the US (but less so overseas), typically features pumpkin additions alongside even more prominent spices: nutmeg, cinnamon, ginger, and cloves are all common. In Belgium, on the other hand, dark and heady Christmas beers tend to feature nutmeg alongside orange peel, vanilla, and other add-ins, and, with their lofty ABVs, make perfect winter warmers.

PORTERS AND STOUTS

What's the difference between a porter and a stout?—(a) very little or (b) it depends on who you talk to. Generally, it comes down to the malt—porters tend to be made from malted barley, while stouts also feature unmalted roasted barley in their grain bills. You're likely

to find that stouts are a little bit stronger, roastier, and heavier on the coffee notes than porters, which tend to be lighter-bodied and veer toward the chocolatey. However, there are many exceptions to this rule—in the world of craft beer, rules are made to be broken.

Sitting under the "porters and stouts" banner are numerous sub-styles. **Porters** can be **robust** (roasty, malty, and full-flavored); **brown** (softer, sweeter, and less boozy); or **Baltic** (brewed with lager yeast—see Chapter 2 Lagers, page 53).

A dry or Irish stout is a very dark, roasty beer with a restrained, coffee-like finish. A **milk stout**, on the other hand, is sweet and creamy with added body from the addition of lactose. **Oatmeal stouts**, unsurprisingly, contain oatmeal in the grain bill, which makes for an incredibly smooth mouthfeel and a touch of sweetness. And **oyster stouts** do indeed contain oysters, most of the time. They are a wonderful throwback to the 19th century, when oysters were cheap and plentiful in London and people ate them by the bucketload at their local taverns. At some point, brewers discovered that the shells (full of calcium carbonate) helped with fining, or clarifying, their beers, after which the shells—followed at some point by the oyster flesh itself—made their way into the brew. The result is a rich, full-bodied, sometimes subtly saline beer—though you shouldn't actually be able to taste the seafood.

Both porters and stouts come in supersized versions—double or imperial strength. **Imperial stouts** are often known as **Russian imperial stouts**, after the old story about Peter the Great wanting to take some stout back home from England. To prepare the beer for its long journey, it was fortified with extra hops and malt, boosting the alcohol content. Whether it's true or not, the style not only survives, but thrives today. These "impies" can be big and roasty, sweet and sticky, or barrel-aged in old wine or spirit casks. As Omnipollo proves, if you can dream it, you can stick it in a beer.

DARK BELGIAN STYLES

Naturally, the Belgians do dark beers extremely well. With roots in Trappist brewing traditions, dubbels and quadrupels are both rich, malty beers. A dubbel is fruity and spicy, full-bodied with often lively carbonation. Its big brother, the quadrupel (or quad), is much stronger, sweeter, and boozier. Quadrupels are sometimes equated with Belgian strong dark ales and sometimes described as a distinct style, depending on whose metric you follow; in either case, they share significant overlap.

OTHER HISTORICAL BRITISH STYLES

The Brits excel at malty styles. Old ales, Scotch ales (aka "wee heavies"), and barley wines are identified as separate styles by many beer rating and judging websites, but the debate goes on in online beer forums and around pub tables as to what the specific differences are. All are lusciously malty—warming, chewy, toffee-like—and fruity, even vinous. As a general rule, a barley wine is likely to be stronger and sweeter. Old ales are brewed with aging in mind, as opposed to milds, which traditionally signify younger, fresher beers. (Pubs would historically keep both and serve a blend mixed to the customer's taste.) A mild is malty rather than hoppy, as an English bitter would be, and generally served on cask, although some bottled versions do exist. Extra Special Bitters (ESBs) probably deserve a shout out here, too. These tend to be darker than normal bitters, with more pronounced malt.

A SIMPLE LIFE—THE KERNEL BREWERY, LONDON

I remember bumping into Evin O'Riordain (below), the founder of London's celebrated Kernel Brewery, at Manchester's Indy Man Beer Con festival a few years ago. Glenn and I had just been to the Buxton x Omnipollo bar to get one of their infamous soft-serve stouts: a big, sweet imperial stout topped with soft-serve ice cream, marshmallows, and nuts. The look on Evin's face was priceless: hell would freeze over before The Kernel started putting nuts on its beers. This is the beauty of the international craft beer scene: there's something for everyone, and plenty of room for disparate approaches. In a world of fast growth and huge hype, The Kernel has taken a different tack—one of quiet focus, operating on its own terms and brewing beers that are rooted in tradition, but which are anything but boring.

Each of The Kernel's beers is packaged with the same plain, brown-paper-bag-style label or tap badge—branding that hasn't changed much since the brewery launched in 2010. Consistency is what The Kernel is famous for—while the hops used may change on a weekly basis, according to availability and the brewers' desires, the beers all meet the same high standard. You know that if you're drinking a Kernel Pale Ale or an Export India Porter, whatever the hops, it will still taste largely like the beer you know and love while showcasing its unique ingredients.

The Kernel is also first and foremost a London brewery, celebrating in its own way the long and illustrious tradition of brewing in the UK capital. While their hoppy beers celebrate the best of modern American brewing, when it comes to dark beers, Evin and his team love to revive long-forgotten London recipes. Their Export Stout is based on an 1890 Truman Brewery recipe; their Imperial Brown Stout on an 1856 recipe from Barclay Perkins.

Evin says: "What I love about beer is how it expresses its sense of place. Our dark beers come rooted in London—the home of dark beers, where they evolved first and became pre-eminent. They are almost all based on 19th-century London recipes (from relatively straight renditions to modernized reworkings), so the place is already there in their inception: the brewery the recipe comes from, its place in London brewing history, the year it was brewed, and what was happening in the world back then."

ESSENTIAL KERNEL BEERS

• Export India Porter: This is HB&B's best-selling dark beer—it's thick, dark, and roasty. We were recently reminded of its magnificence when we poured a glass at a photoshoot for this book. More than an hour later, we came back to find that the glass looked exactly the same as when we'd poured it. Now that's head retention…
• Imperial Brown Stout: Checking in generally at around 9.6% ABV, this big beer delivers a ridiculously smooth hit of espresso roast, dark fruits, and chocolate. If it were a cocktail, we'd call it Corpse Reviver No. Brew.

EVIN'S PERFECT PAIRING

"Dark beers' maltiness, roastiness, or sweetness can provide a very good foil for a wide spread of different foods, but I'll stick with what I know: cheese. Traditional British territorial cheese with traditional British beer, namely porters and stouts. With Cheshire. With Stichelton. With Montgomery's Cheddar."

FOOD PAIRINGS

As dark beers comprise such an enormous range, they also offer ample opportunities for food pairings. Dry Irish stouts and brown ales do well to temper spicy dishes; smoky rauchbiers are a dream with barbecued meat and spiced pumpkin; Christmas beers can suit sweet and savory preparations; and wide-ranging porters and stouts can stand up to game meats, rich stews, enormous roasts, and other indulgent fare. Don't forget, too, about dark beers' way with dessert: many porters and stouts are improved with a scoop of vanilla ice cream, taste exquisite with chocolate, and are a natural pairing for cookies. Meanwhile, Belgian and British styles, such as old ales and quadrupels, lend themselves to apples, caramel, and dried fruit.

STYLE	CHARACTERISTICS	PAIR WITH
Brown ale	Malty, nutty, caramel	Kimchi and eggplant (aubergine) stir-fry, sumac-braised chicken thighs
Altbier	Nutty, peppery, toasty	Cured meats, steak salad, caramel apple strudel
Smoked beer/rauchbier	Rich, smoky, toasty	Carnitas, bacon, mint chocolate mousse
Pumpkin beer	Spicy, sweet, amber	Pumpkin risotto, pumpkin pie, roasted butternut squash
Christmas beer	Spicy, rich, warming	Prime rib, mince pies, glazed ham
Porter		
Robust porter	Roasty, malty, full-flavored	Blue cheese, beef stew
Brown porter	Soft, sweet, mid-strength	Polenta with truffle cheese and mushrooms, Reuben sandwich
Baltic porter	Dark, sweet, roasty	Hearty stews, barbecued beef, cheesecake
Imperial porter	Dark, chocolate, full-bodied	Brownies, pasta with rich meat ragù
Stout		
Dry Irish stout	Dry, roasty, coffee	Mole poblano, lobster and scallops, ham
Milk stout	Sweet, creamy, chocolate	Vanilla ice cream, chocolate desserts
Oatmeal stout	Sweet, creamy, smooth	Oatmeal chocolate chip cookies, triple crème cheese
Oyster stout	Rich, full-bodied, roasty	Oysters on the half-shell, fried oyster po'boy
Russian imperial stout	High ABV, roasty or sweet, sticky	Venison steaks with chocolate sauce, blueberry and blackberry cobbler
Old ale	Toffee, chewy, vinous	Roast duck, apple crumble
Scotch ale	Toffee, chewy, tea-like	Game birds, slow-roasted leg of lamb
Barley wine	Sweet, chewy, boozy	Baked macaroni and cheese, aged Gouda
Dubbel	Fruity, spicy, carbonated	Roasted spiced quails, braised short ribs
Quadrupel	Strong, sweet, spicy	Maple raisin bread pudding, braised oxtail

ROAST TOMATO, PEPPER, AND GARLIC SOUP

2lb (900g) plum tomatoes, halved

2–3 large red bell (sweet) peppers, halved, de-stemmed, and deseeded

1 large head garlic

4 tbsps olive oil, divided, plus extra for drizzling

1 large onion, diced

Thumb-sized piece of fresh ginger, peeled and grated or finely minced

2 tsps ground cumin

1½ tsps smoked paprika

2 cups (500ml) vegetable stock

½ tbsp sherry vinegar

1 tbsp light brown sugar

1 tbsp fresh thyme leaves, roughly chopped, plus extra to garnish

Fine sea salt and freshly ground black pepper

Poached eggs (optional) and crusty bread, to serve

SERVES 4 TO 5 AS A STARTER OR 2 TO 3 AS A MAIN

Make this soup at the cusp of autumn: when tomatoes are still in season, but there is a distinct chill in the air. Top each bowl with a just-cooked poached egg for additional richness, or leave it out if you want to make the dish vegan. Serve alongside a hunk of crusty bread—all the better to soak up every last drop.

PAIR WITH A rauchbier or other smoky style. Rauchbiers (meaning "smoke beers") hail from Bavaria and Franconia; their kindled flavor is down to the malt being roasted over beechwood fires. The result is a beer with an aroma that's reminiscent of a campfire, and a savory edge. They're perfect for autumn drinking, pairing well with this smoky soup.

THREE BEERS TO TRY Five Points London Smoke (UK); Schlenkerla Märzen (Germany); Sly Fox Rauch Bier (US)

1 Preheat the oven to 400°F/200°C/Gas 6. Line a large baking sheet with foil. Place the halved tomatoes, cut side up, and the peppers, cut side down, on the sheet. (You may need to use two baking sheets; the vegetables should lie flat without any overlap.)

2 Slice off the top of the garlic stem, but leave the head intact. Pour a drop of olive oil into the center, wrap tightly in foil, and place on the baking sheet. Drizzle 2 tablespoons of olive oil over the tomatoes and peppers, and season well with sea salt and pepper.

3 Roast the vegetables for 45 minutes to 1 hour, pausing to rotate the baking sheet(s) halfway through. Roast until the tomatoes are darkened and just charred at the edges, and the peppers are well charred. Remove from the oven and cool for 5 minutes.

4 Once cool enough to handle, remove the skin from the peppers and discard. Tear the peppers into small strips. Unwrap the garlic bulb; it should be softened and sticky. Separate each clove and squeeze the softened, roasted garlic into a ramekin.

5 To prepare the soup base, add the remaining 2 tablespoons of olive oil to a large saucepan with a lid, and place over medium-high heat. Once the oil is hot, add the onion and season to taste with sea salt. Cook, stirring frequently, for 5–6 minutes, or until softened. Add the ginger and cook, stirring often, for 4–5 minutes, or until the raw smell dissipates. Add the cumin and paprika, and cook for about 30 seconds.

6 Add the roast tomatoes and peppers, and any accumulated juices, to the pan, along with the garlic paste. Pour over the vegetable stock and stir in the vinegar and sugar. Remove from the heat and, using an immersion blender or food processor, pulse until the soup is thickened and chunky, but not completely smooth.

7 Return the pot to the heat and add the thyme leaves. Bring the soup to a boil, then cover and reduce to a simmer. Cook for approximately 30 minutes, or until the soup has thickened and is slightly darkened in color. Season to taste.

8 Divide the soup into bowls and garnish with more thyme leaves and a drizzle of olive oil. Top each soup with a poached egg, if you like, and serve with crusty bread.

CARNITAS TACOS WITH TOMATILLO GUACAMOLE

3lb (1.3kg) rind-on pork shoulder

3 tsps fine sea salt

2 tsps ground cumin

1 tsp dried oregano (preferably Mexican)

3 bay leaves

1 large onion, sliced into large wedges

6 garlic cloves, smashed

1 orange, halved

2/3 cup (150ml) vegetable oil

10–12 small corn tortillas

FOR THE TOMATILLO GUACAMOLE

6 tomatillos (about 14oz/400g), husks removed and rinsed

1/2 red onion, finely diced

Large bunch of cilantro (fresh coriander), roughly chopped

1–2 jalapeños, finely chopped

2 large, very ripe avocados

1 tsp fine sea salt

Juice of 1 lime

TO GARNISH

Additional cilantro (fresh coriander)

Lime wedges

SERVES 4 TO 5

Traditionally, carnitas—Mexican-style pork shoulder, which is slow-cooked, shredded and then crisped up—are cooked in buckets of lard, which most home cooks don't seem to have going spare these days. Some contemporary recipes get around the lard factor by braising the pork, which works in a pinch, but doesn't quite achieve the same melting, unctuous texture. Credit the genius of J. Kenji López-Alt, then; he opts to confit his carnitas in vegetable oil instead, which is a technique I riff on here. The result is easy enough to do at home, extraordinarily tender, and can be the basis for any at-home taco party. Don't forget the vividly green tomatillo guacamole to accompany.

PAIR WITH A smoky stout or porter. After the carnitas are confited, they're shredded and quickly broiled (grilled) to achieve a crisp, golden brown exterior. In this like-with-like pairing, the beer's roasty malt profile, plus its smokiness, are a perfect complement to the meat.

THREE BEERS TO TRY DEYA Taill Dragger Porter (UK); Stillwater Artisanal Ready Made: Vacuum (US); Surly Smoke (US)

1 Preheat the oven to 275°F/140°C/Gas 1. Remove the rind (the skin and thick layer of fat) from the pork shoulder. Separate the fat from the skin and set aside (discard or save the skin to make chicharrones). Dice approximately 7oz (200g) of the fat into small cubes (save the rest for other cooking projects or discard). Cut the pork shoulder meat into roughly 1½-inch (4cm) cubes and add to a bowl, along with the cubed fat. Season with the sea salt, cumin, and oregano, and toss to coat evenly.

2 Transfer the pork shoulder and fat to a medium-sized baking dish, roughly 9 x 13 inches (23 x 33cm) and preferably made from Pyrex or ceramic, and stir through the bay leaves, onion wedges, and garlic until evenly distributed (the pork pieces should be tightly packed in). Squeeze over the orange halves, then add them to the dish. Pour over the vegetable oil; the pork should be nearly submerged to confit properly. If necessary, pour in more oil until it nearly reaches the top of the meat. Cover tightly with foil and bake for 3–3½ hours, or until the pork is fork-tender. Remove the pork from the oven and let cool.

3 Meanwhile, to make the guacamole, preheat the broiler (grill) to high. Remove the cores from the tomatillos, but otherwise leave them whole. Line a small baking sheet with foil and broil the tomatillos for 6–8 minutes, or until softened and starting to char on top. Flip the tomatillos over with tongs and cook for a further 5–6 minutes, or until completely softened and darkened on the other side. Remove from the broiler and let cool for several minutes.

4 Once the tomatillos are cool enough to handle, chop roughly and add to a medium-sized bowl. Stir through the onion, cilantro (fresh coriander), and jalapeños.

5 Halve and pit (stone) each avocado with a sharp knife. Cut a crosshatch pattern into each half to dice, scoop out with a spoon, and add to the bowl. Stir in the sea salt and lime juice. If the avocado is still a little on the firm side, mash lightly with a fork. Cover and set aside.

6 Shortly before serving, use a slotted spoon to transfer the pork, fat, and garlic to a clean baking sheet lined with foil. Use two forks or your hands to shred the pork pieces. Broil (grill) on high for approximately 4–5 minutes, or until the pork is browned and crisp. Remove from the broiler, toss the pork so the browned parts aren't exposed, and cook for a further 3–4 minutes.

7 While the pork is broiling, place a large skillet (frying pan) over medium-low heat and add as many tortillas as can fit comfortably. Cook the tortillas for 1–2 minutes on each side, or until warmed and just beginning to turn golden. Transfer to a plate and cover with a paper towel. Repeat for the remaining tortillas.

8 Let diners build their own tacos: serve the pork, guacamole, and tortillas simultaneously, plus extra cilantro and lime wedges to garnish.

CHINESE GLAZED BABY BACK RIBS

1 rack (about 3lb/1.3kg) baby back ribs, trimmed and cut into individual riblets

1 tbsp Chinese five-spice powder

½ cup (125ml) hoisin sauce

3 tbsps soy sauce

3 tbsps clear honey

1 tbsp rice vinegar

1½ tbsps sesame oil

1 tbsp Shaoxing rice wine or sake

4 garlic cloves, finely chopped

Thumb-sized piece of fresh ginger, peeled and finely chopped

2–3 spicy red chili peppers, such as bird's-eye, finely chopped, plus extra to garnish (optional)

2–3 scallions (spring onions), thinly sliced, to garnish

SERVES 4

Ribs tend to conjure images of sweat-streaked pitmasters and smoke-clogged barbecues. Fair enough, then, if you've ever hesitated to make them at home, but note that these ribs require none of those pyrotechnics—or even a broiler (grill)—to achieve bold flavor and real tenderness. All they need, in fact, is to marinate for 24 hours in the refrigerator and then cook low and slow in the oven. There are very few limits as far as marinade ingredients are concerned, but I like this Chinese-inspired version, which blends the funk of hoisin, saline soy sauce, fragrant five-spice powder, and sweet honey.

PAIR WITH A schwarzbier. Schwarzbiers—which tranlates to "black beers"—traditionally hail from central and east Germany, and are brewed with dark-roasted malts and lager yeast. That combination of roasty toasty flavors with refreshing drinkability works a treat alongside these rich, burnished ribs.

THREE BEERS TO TRY Anspach & Hobday Das Schwarzbier (UK); Bohem Brewery Druid (UK); Suarez Family Bones Shirt (US)

1 Start marinating the ribs 24 hours before cooking. Add the ribs and five-spice powder to a large Ziploc bag or nonreactive bowl, and toss until evenly coated.

2 Mix together the hoisin sauce, soy sauce, honey, rice vinegar, sesame oil, Shaoxing rice wine or sake, garlic, ginger, and chili peppers in a small bowl. Pour the sauce over the ribs and shake or mix to coat evenly. Seal the bag or cover the bowl, and chill in the refrigerator for 24 hours.

3 Preheat the oven to 300°F/150°C/Gas 2. Line a large baking sheet with foil and put a wire rack on top. Remove the ribs from the marinade and place in a single layer on the rack (return the marinade to the refrigerator). Cover the ribs tightly with foil and cook in the oven for 1 hour.

4 Remove the ribs from the oven and brush with half of the remaining marinade. Cover and cook for a further 20–30 minutes, or until the ribs are completely fork-tender. Flip with tongs and brush on the remaining marinade, then cook, uncovered, for a final 5 minutes, or until the ribs are dark and sticky.

5 Once the ribs are fully cooked, let cool for 10 minutes. Garnish with the sliced red chilis (if using) and scallions (spring onions) and serve.

BUTTERNUT SQUASH RISOTTO

1 small butternut squash (about 2lb/900g)

4 tbsps olive oil, divided

1 large onion, finely diced

4 garlic cloves, finely chopped

1½ cups (300g) Arborio rice

4½ cups (1 liter) chicken stock, plus extra if needed

1 cup (250ml) dry white wine

3 tbsps (45g) unsalted butter

20 fresh sage leaves

¾ cup (75g) shaved Parmigiano Reggiano, plus extra to serve

Fine sea salt and freshly ground black pepper

Nutmeg, preferably freshly grated, to serve

SERVES 4 TO 5

There are a lot of myths about risotto, the most persistent being that it is necessary to stir it constantly as it cooks (given that risotto takes 30–40 minutes to make, that's a lot of armwork). Other recipes advocate a totally hands-off approach, leaving the rice and liquid to simmer together undisturbed. I prefer a method that's somewhere in the middle. By keeping the heat low, including several large additions of liquid, and stirring occasionally rather than constantly, the result is rich and creamy without being sticky and overworked. Add cubes of butternut squash, a grating of nutmeg, and fried sage leaves to lend this risotto a particularly autumnal appeal.

PAIR WITH A pumpkin beer. There are a lot of iterations out there these days (likely more so in the US, the spiritual home of the style, than other places), from pumpkin-coffee stouts to pumpkin-flavored lagers. Here, go for a classic version of the style—perhaps one with just enough hoppy bitterness to stand up to the risotto's richness.

THREE BEERS TO TRY River Horse Brewing Hipp-o-Lantern Imperial Pumpkin Ale (US); Southern Tier Imperial Pumking (US); Two Roads Roadsmary's Baby (US)

1 First, prepare the squash. Slice off the top and bottom, and remove the skin using a chef's knife or strong peeler. Slice in half lengthwise, scoop out the seeds, and cut into roughly ½-inch (1cm) cubes. Set aside.

2 Add 2 tablespoons of the olive oil to a large, deep skillet (frying pan) and place over medium-high heat. Once the oil is hot, add the squash and season well with sea salt and black pepper. Sauté the squash until just fork-tender and beginning to brown (about 10–12 minutes). Transfer the squash to a bowl and set aside.

3 Wipe out the skillet and return to the stovetop. Add the remaining olive oil and place over medium-high heat. Once the oil is hot, add the onion and cook, stirring frequently, for approximately 5 minutes, or until softened and beginning to turn translucent. Add the garlic and cook for 1 minute more.

4 Add the dry rice to the skillet and stir until evenly coated with oil. Cook for 2–3 minutes, or until lightly toasted. Pour over roughly half the stock, or until the rice is just covered with the liquid. Bring to a boil, then reduce to a simmer. Cook, stirring occasionally, until most of the stock is absorbed.

5 Add the wine and half the remaining stock. Add half the squash at this stage; it will start to melt into the risotto. Keep the risotto at a simmer, stirring occasionally to encourage creaminess and stop it sticking to the skillet.

6 Meanwhile, melt the butter in a small skillet (frying pan) over medium-high heat. Once the butter has just melted, but before it starts to foam, add the sage leaves in a single layer. Fry the leaves for about 3 minutes, or until they are crispy and the butter is browned, but not burned—watch attentively, as this process happens quickly. Remove from the heat and set aside.

7 Once most of the liquid has been absorbed, add the remainder of the stock to the risotto. Cook, stirring frequently, until the risotto is thick and creamy, and the rice still has just a bit of bite. Stir through the remainder of the squash. Season to taste. If the rice is still a bit too al dente for your taste, or if you prefer risotto on the thinner side, add more stock a little at a time.

8 When the risotto is ready, remove the skillet from the heat and add the Parmigiano Reggiano. Drain the browned butter from the sage leaves and fold through the risotto.

9 Divide the risotto between plates. Top with a good grating of nutmeg, a generous amount of Parmigiano Reggiano, and the fried sage leaves. Serve immediately.

BLUE CHEESE MACARONI

1lb (450g) cavatappi or elbow macaroni

1 12fl oz (350ml) can evaporated milk

1 tbsp cornstarch (cornflour)

2 tbsps cold water

3½ tbsps (50g) unsalted butter

3¾ cups (375g) grated medium white Cheddar cheese

11oz (310g) creamy blue cheese (preferably Gorgonzola dolce), rind removed and sliced into small pieces

Fine sea salt

Tabasco sauce and 1 red chili pepper, thinly sliced, to serve (optional)

SERVES 5 TO 6

There are two camps when it comes to macaroni and cheese: some favor the oven-baked version, which is typically made with a béchamel sauce and topped with breadcrumbs. Others prefer stovetop mac 'n' cheese, which is almost endlessly gooey and comforting. I fall in the latter camp. This recipe, to me, is everything I want from the dish. To add a surprising, adult twist, I like to use a creamy blue cheese alongside the white Cheddar (preferably Gorgonzola dolce, which is so soft it's often sold in tubs). Really, though, you can use any meltable cheeses that you like.

PAIR WITH A stout or barley wine. Blue cheese and stout or porter is a famously excellent pairing, and it works just as well in macaroni and cheese form. A boozy, malt-driven barley wine also makes a fine choice with this indulgent dish.

THREE BEERS TO TRY AleSmith Old Numbskull (US); J.W. Lees Harvest Ale (UK); North Coast Old Rasputin (US)

1 Bring a large saucepan of generously salted water to the boil. Add the pasta and cook according to the directions on the packet or until just al dente.

2 Meanwhile, add the evaporated milk to a small saucepan and place over medium-low heat. Heat until warmed through, but not boiling or scalded. Add the cornstarch (cornflour) and water to a small bowl, and whisk until uniform. Stir the cornstarch mixture through the milk.

3 Once cooked, drain the pasta and return to the large saucepan. Stir through the butter until completely melted. Pour in the milk mixture and add both cheeses. Stir through rapidly until the cheeses melt and the sauce becomes thick, creamy, and uniform.

4 Divide between bowls and serve immediately. If you'd like a bit of extra kick, serve with a few dashes of Tabasco and some sliced chili.

TRUFFLE CHEESE POLENTA WITH MUSHROOM

1½ cups (350ml) chicken or vegetable stock

⅓ cup (50g) quick-cooking polenta

4½ oz (125g) semi-soft, truffle-flavored cheese (such as sottocenere)

4 tbsps (60g) unsalted butter, divided

10½ oz (300g) mini portobello mushrooms

2 garlic cloves, lightly smashed

1 tbsp fresh thyme leaves, roughly chopped, plus extra to garnish

2 duck eggs

Fine sea salt and freshly ground black pepper

SERVES 2

In deepest, darkest winter, there's always polenta to bring some sun. Golden yellow on the plate, it's incredibly quick and easy to make (provided you buy the fast-cooking version). Because cold weather requires indulgence, the polenta is folded through with butter and truffle-scented cheese before being topped with nutty portobello mushrooms and the meaty perfection of a fried duck egg.

PAIR WITH A smooth, roasty porter. Here, the mushrooms and truffle cheese both thrum with deep, rich umami flavors—ones which are flattered by a dose of roasty malt.

THREE BEERS TO TRY Hill Farmstead Everett (US); The Kernel Export India Porter (UK); Yeastie Boys Pot Kettle Black (NZ)

1 First, prepare the polenta. Heat the stock in a medium saucepan until just boiling. Add the polenta in a steady stream, whisking continuously, to prevent it clumping. Keep whisking until the mixture thickens (about 3–5 minutes).

2 Meanwhile, remove the rind from the cheese and slice as thinly as possible. Add 1 tablespoon (15g) of butter to the polenta and all but a few shavings of the cheese (you'll use these to garnish the dish). Whisk well until uniform, and season to taste with sea salt. Remove from the heat, cover, and set aside.

3 Prepare the mushrooms by discarding the stems, then remove any dirt with a paper towel or brush (don't use any water, it will make them soggy). Once cleaned, slice thinly.

4 Place a large, heavy-bottomed skillet (frying pan)—preferably made from cast iron—over high heat. Once very hot, add 1 tablespoon (15g) of the butter and, as soon as it melts, add half the mushrooms and all the garlic, and spread in an even layer. Cook without disturbing for 2–3 minutes; you want the mushrooms to turn a deep golden brown. Flip and cook further until the mushrooms are golden on all sides. Transfer to a bowl and repeat with the remaining batch of mushrooms, adding a second tablespoon (15g) of butter to the skillet. Once all the mushrooms are cooked, season to taste with sea salt and black pepper, and stir through the thyme leaves.

5 Just before serving, return the pan of polenta to a low heat. If it has started to solidify, whisk through a couple of tablespoons of hot water or extra stock.

6 Meanwhile, fry the duck eggs. Wipe out the skillet and place over medium-low heat. Add the remaining tablespoon (15g) of butter. Once the butter has melted and the skillet is warm, crack both eggs into the pan. Cook, using a spatula to ensure the eggs don't stick, for approximately 4 minutes, or until the whites are cooked through and yolks still runny. Remove from the heat.

7 To serve, divide the polenta between two plates and top with the mushrooms. Garnish with the extra shavings of cheese, more thyme leaves, and the fried duck eggs. Season the eggs lightly with salt and pepper, and serve immediately.

ROAST QUAIL AND SQUASH WITH YOGURT SAUCE AND HAZELNUT GREMOLATA

4 quails

1½ tsps fine sea salt

5 tbsps olive oil

1 tbsp ground cumin

2 tsps ground coriander

1 tsp ground allspice

1 tsp ground cloves

1 tsp ground nutmeg

1 tsp ground ginger

2 tbsps pomegranate
molasses

1½ tbsps clear honey

2 tsps rose water

Zest and juice of 1 orange

2 tsps sambal oelek hot
sauce (optional)

FOR THE YOGURT
SAUCE

1½ tbsps (20g) unsalted
butter

½ cup (115g) Greek yogurt,
at room temperature

2–3 tbsps cold water

Pinch of flaky sea salt
(such as Maldon)

FOR THE SQUASH

1 small kabocha, red kuri,
or baby hubbard squash
(or another similar, thin-
skinned variety)

3–4 tbsps olive oil

Flaky sea salt and freshly
ground black pepper

*(Ingredients continue
overleaf)*

I love the look of quail on a plate: each small bird resembles a perfect, miniature chicken. Quails are juicy when cooked right, but—as a lean meat—become dry when overcooked. Two ways to increase their succulence are marinating them overnight (I favor a Middle Eastern-style marinade here, rich with spice, piquant pomegranate molasses, and zesty orange juice) and spatchcocking (or butterflying) them: by removing their backbones and pressing them flat, they roast quickly and evenly. Make a feast of it: serve your quail with roasted winter squash, and top with a browned butter yogurt sauce and hazelnut gremolata for freshness.

PAIR WITH A dark Belgian style, like a dubbel or quad. Belgian yeast is known for its fruity, spicy characteristics. Here, those traits play well with the deeply spiced marinade, while the dark malt profile picks up the roasted notes of the quail and squash.

THREE BEERS TO TRY Brasseri de Rochefort Trappistes Rochefort 8 (Belgium); Brouwerij Westvleteren Westvleteren 8 (Belgium); Deschutes Brewery The Stoic (US)

1 Begin prepping the night before cooking. First, spatchcock the quails: use kitchen shears to snip all the way along one side of the spine and then the other. Discard the backbones (or save for a stock), flip the quails over, and flatten by pressing gently on the breastbones. Generously season both sides of each quail with sea salt. Set aside.

2 To make the marinade, whisk the olive oil and all the spices together in a large nonreactive bowl. Whisk in the pomegranate molasses, honey, rose water, and orange zest and juice. Mix in the sambal oelek hot sauce (if using). Transfer the quails to the bowl and arrange so they are as submerged in the marinade as possible. Cover and chill in the refrigerator overnight.

3 The next day, remove the quails from the fridge about 1 hour before cooking to come to room temperature.

4 Meanwhile, to make the yogurt sauce, add the butter to a small skillet (frying pan) over medium-high heat. Cook for approximately 3 minutes, or until the butter has melted, turned dark amber, and smells nutty (watch closely as the butter will brown quickly). Once the butter is browned, remove from the heat and transfer immediately to a heatproof bowl. Chill for 30–45 minutes, or until cool but not solidified.

5 Preheat the oven to 350°F/180°C/Gas 4. Next, prepare the squash. Wash off any dirt and pat dry. Slice off the stem and then cut in half (no peeling necessary). Scoop out the seeds and gunk from the cavity, and discard. Slice the squash into roughly 1-inch (2.5cm) crescents.

(Method continues overleaf)

2 tbsps blanched
hazelnuts

Large bunch of fresh
mint leaves

Large bunch of cilantro
(fresh coriander)

Zest of 1 lemon

1 garlic clove, peeled

½ tsp fine sea salt

SERVES 2 TO 4

6 Line a large baking sheet with parchment (baking) paper and arrange the squash in a single layer. Drizzle over the olive oil and season with sea salt and black pepper. Flip the slices over and season on the other side. Drizzle over several spoonfuls of the marinade.

7 Line a second large baking sheet with foil and place a wire rack on top. Remove the quails from the marinade and arrange on the rack; they should be breast-side up with legs splayed (this helps them cook quickly and evenly). Spoon over more marinade.

8 Roast the squash in the oven for approximately 20–30 minutes, or until fork-tender. Halfway through, add the quails to the oven and roast for about 18 minutes, or until the marinade has darkened and they are just cooked through (it's fine, even preferable, if they're a little bit pink in the center).

9 Meanwhile, to make the gremolata, add the hazelnuts to a food processor and pulse until finely chopped. Add the remaining ingredients and pulse until finely mixed and uniform. (You can also use a mortar and pestle, if you prefer.) Set aside.

10 When the quails and squash are cooked, finish the yogurt sauce by adding the yogurt to a bowl and pouring in the cooled browned butter in a slow, steady stream, whisking constantly to combine. Add the water, 1 tablespoon at a time, and whisk between additions, until the sauce reaches your preferred consistency—it should be thin enough to drizzle. Season to taste with the flaky sea salt.

11 To serve, divide the squash slices between plates and allocate one quail per person (two if you're especially hungry). Drizzle over the yogurt sauce and top with the hazelnut gremolata.

BEER-BRAISED SHORT RIBS

I don't normally recommend cooking with beer, but these short ribs are an exception. The Belgians long ago determined that malty, dark beers are lovely in hearty stews, and this recipe takes inspiration from the classic carbonnade à la flamande. Ribboned with fat, and phenomenally unctuous, short ribs are also one of the most budget-friendly cuts of beef you can buy. To cook them properly, you need to braise them for several hours until much of the fat renders and the meat begins to slip off the bone. Ask your butcher for flanken-cut short ribs (rather than English-cut), which consist of a long, thin strip that can be separated into individual rib segments.

PAIR WITH A Belgian dubbel. Buy a few bottles to use in the braise, and an extra to go alongside. Rich, deep, and dark, it's as good in the glass as it is in the saucepan.

THREE BEERS TO TRY Lost Abbey Lost & Found (US); New Belgium Abbey (US); Westmalle Dubbel (Belgium)

3lb (1.3kg) short ribs, flanken cut and separated into individual rib segments

2 tbsps (30g) unsalted butter

1–2 tbsps olive oil

3 large onions, thickly sliced

3½ cups (850ml) Belgian dubbel, divided

5½ oz (155g) bacon lardons or pancetta

3 garlic cloves, smashed

2 medium carrots, halved and thinly sliced

3 tbsps tomato paste (purée)

3 tbsps molasses (black treacle)

2 bay leaves

Fine sea salt

Boiled or mashed potatoes, or cooked egg noodles, to serve

Small bunch of fresh parsley, chopped, to garnish

FOR THE MARINADE

1 tbsp flaky sea salt (such as Maldon)

1 tsp freshly ground black pepper

2 tsps ground allspice

3 tbsps olive oil

4 garlic cloves, finely chopped

SERVES 4

1 Marinate the ribs about 1 hour before cooking. Place the ribs in a bowl, sprinkle over the sea salt, black pepper, and allspice for the marinade, and toss to coat. Stir through the olive oil and garlic. Place the ribs in the fridge to marinate.

2 While the ribs are marinating, caramelize the onions. Add the butter and olive oil to a large skillet (frying pan) over medium-high heat. Once the butter has melted, add the onions, toss to coat, and reduce the heat to low. Cook for 30–40 minutes, stirring occasionally, until the onions are deep golden brown, but not scorched on the outsides. Add ½ cup (125ml) of the beer and cook off until mostly evaporated. Remove from the heat and set aside.

3 Preheat the oven to 325°F/160°C/Gas 3. Add a small splash of olive oil to a Dutch oven, or flameproof casserole dish, and place over medium-high heat. Once the oil is hot, add the lardons or pancetta, garlic, and carrots. Cook for 8–10 minutes, or until the lardons are starting to crisp and darken and the carrots are tender. Transfer to a bowl.

4 Increase the heat to high. Place half the ribs in the cooking pot, sear on each side until golden brown (about 8–10 minutes in total), and transfer to a plate. Repeat with the second batch of ribs.

5 Reduce the heat to medium-low and pour 2½ cups (625ml) of the beer into the pot. Use a wooden spoon to scrape up any tasty brown bits from the bottom. Add the caramelized onions and the carrot and lardon mixture to the pot. Add the tomato paste (purée), molasses (black treacle), and bay leaves, and stir through to combine. Season to taste with sea salt. Return the ribs to the pot and immerse in as much of the liquid as possible. Cover and transfer to the oven.

6 Cook for approximately 3 hours, or until the ribs are completely tender and the meat is falling off the bone. Using tongs, carefully transfer the ribs to a bowl (removing and discarding the bones if still attached). The ribs will have released a lot of fat—using a sieve, carefully strain off what's left in the pot. Save the solids (except the bay leaves) and discard the fat when it has cooled.

7 Return the solids to a small skillet (frying pan) and add the remaining ½ cup (125ml) of beer. Cook over medium heat for a few minutes until the beer has mostly evaporated. Pour over the reserved ribs. You can either serve the short ribs right away or, if you can bear it, chill in the refrigerator overnight, reheat, and serve the next day, to allow the flavors to deepen further.

8 Serve with boiled or mashed potatoes, egg noodles, or another carb of your choice, and garnish with the parsley.

VENISON STEAKS WITH DARK CHOCOLATE SAUCE

2 venison steaks (about 8½ oz/240g each)

1 tbsp olive oil

Flaky sea salt (such as Maldon)

Roasted new potatoes and salad leaves (optional), to serve

FOR THE CHOCOLATE SAUCE

2 tbsps (30g) unsalted butter

2 echalion (banana) shallots, finely chopped

2 garlic cloves, smashed

½ cup (125ml) rich red wine

1½ cups (350ml) beef stock

1 bay leaf

½ oz (15g) semi-sweet (dark) chocolate (minimum 70% cocoa solids)

Fine sea salt and freshly ground black pepper

SERVES 2

Rich, ferric venison is a meat for true carnivores—I relish it, particularly during the long winter months. Despite its intensity of flavor, venison is a famously lean meat, so be sure to cook it rare, or medium-rare at most—any more and it becomes unpalatably chewy. Venison and chocolate might sound like an odd combination, but the two get along famously; the dark bitterness of the chocolate is a match for the meat's own deep, gamy flavors. Serve roast potatoes on the side to make a feast of it.

PAIR WITH As far as complementary pairings go, it's hard to do better than a chocolate stout and venison with chocolate sauce—the two are perfectly matched in terms of flavor, richness, and intensity. For a slightly contrasting option, go for a raspberry stout, or another stout with fruity flavors.

THREE BEERS TO TRY Bell's Brewery Expedition Stout (US); Burning Sky Cherry Monolith (UK); Kereru Imperial Nibs (NZ)

1 Remove the steaks from the refrigerator about 1 hour before cooking. Season both sides generously with sea salt and let come to room temperature.

2 Meanwhile, to prepare the chocolate sauce, melt the butter in a medium saucepan over medium heat. Once the butter has melted, add the shallots and garlic, season generously with pepper, and cook, stirring frequently, for 5–7 minutes or until softened.

3 Add the red wine to the pan and increase the heat to high. Reduce the wine until it is nearly evaporated. Add the beef stock and bay leaf, and reduce the heat to medium-high. Cook for approximately 20 minutes, or until the sauce reduces by more than half and is thickened and nearly syrupy in consistency. Remove from the heat and strain to remove the shallots, garlic, and bay leaf. Return the sauce to the pan and season to taste. Set aside.

4 Next, cook the steaks. Add the oil to a large skillet (frying pan) over medium-high heat. Once the oil is hot, but not smoking, add the two steaks. Cook for 1 minute, flip, and cook for a further 45 seconds to 1 minute on the other side. If necessary, use tongs to pick up the steaks and sear off the sides. Transfer to a cutting board and let rest for 5 minutes. (If the steaks are more than 1-inch/2.5cm thick, you may want to increase the cooking time by 1–2 minutes in total.)

5 Meanwhile, place the sauce over low heat. Chop the chocolate very finely, add the shavings to the sauce, and whisk through until uniform. Cook until heated through, but be careful not to bring to a boil, as the sauce may split.

6 Place the steaks on serving plates and drizzle with the chocolate sauce. Serve with the roasted new potatoes and few salad leaves (if using).

EGGPLANT STIR-FRY WITH KIMCHI SAUCE

1¼ lb (600g) eggplants
(aubergines), preferably
Japanese or baby
eggplants

1 tbsp fine sea salt

3–4 tbsps vegetable oil,
divided, plus extra if
needed

1 cup (200g) kimchi,
roughly chopped (excess
liquid squeezed out and
retained)

3 scallions (spring onions),
finely diced (white and
green parts separated)

4–5 garlic cloves, finely
chopped

Thumb-sized piece of
fresh ginger, peeled
and finely chopped

FOR THE KIMCHI SAUCE

5 tbsps (75ml) kimchi
juice, from the chopped
kimchi and the container

1½ tbsps gochujang (chili
paste)

1 tbsp toasted sesame oil

1 tbsp soy sauce

1 tbsp Shaoxing rice wine
or mirin

1 tbsp cornstarch
(cornflour)

½ tbsp dark brown sugar

TO SERVE

Steamed rice

4 egg yolks (optional)

Sesame seeds

Small bunch of scallions
(spring onions), finely
sliced

SERVES 4

Thrumming with umami and zippy with heat, this stir-fry is a dish whose relatively simple preparation belies the boldness of its flavors. Look for slender Japanese eggplants (aubergines), or opt for baby eggplants if those aren't available; whichever variety you find, the eggplants should be shiny and firm. Salting them prior to cooking eliminates any bitterness, and also renders them meltingly soft. A generous amount of kimchi, plus gochujang (fermented Korean chili paste), makes this one for chili heads.

PAIR WITH An imperial brown ale or stout. This is a dish with bold flavors and intense spicing; instead of a hoppy style, which would heighten the heat, sweeter, maltier styles lend a cooling effect.

THREE BEERS TO TRY Batch Brewing The Huge Kahuna (Australia); Cigar City Brewing Bolita Double Nut Brown Ale (US); Trillium Deciduous Imperial Brown Ale (US)

1 About 30 minutes before cooking, prep the eggplants (aubergines). Remove the stems, halve, and chop into roughly 1-inch (2.5cm) pieces (don't worry about peeling them). Add the eggplants to a colander and sprinkle over the sea salt. Lightly toss, ensuring the pieces are evenly coated, then let drain and soften for 30 minutes.

2 Rinse the eggplants with cold water and press lightly to drain. Transfer to paper towels and cover with a second layer of paper towels. Press to squeeze out any excess liquid. Let dry for a further 20 minutes.

3 Meanwhile, to prepare the kimchi sauce, add the 5 tablespoons (75ml) of kimchi juice to a bowl. Add the remaining sauce ingredients and whisk until smooth. Set aside.

4 Place a large skillet (frying pan) or wok over high heat and add 2 tablespoons of the vegetable oil. Once the oil is very hot, add half the eggplant, cut sides down, and cook without agitating for 1–2 minutes, or until the pieces start to turn golden brown. Cook, tossing frequently, for a further 2–3 minutes, or until the eggplant is tender and golden. Transfer to a plate and repeat with the second batch, adding more oil if necessary.

5 Return the skillet or wok to the stovetop and add 1 tablespoon of the vegetable oil. Once the oil is very hot, add the chopped kimchi and cook, tossing often, for 3–4 minutes, or until starting to caramelize. Transfer to the plate with the eggplant pieces.

6 Add a dribble of oil to the skillet or wok along with the white parts of the scallions (spring onions), garlic, and ginger. Cook for 1–2 minutes, or until fragrant and starting to turn golden. Return the eggplant and kimchi to the pan, and toss to combine. Reduce the heat to medium-low and add the kimchi sauce and the green parts of the scallions. Toss to combine and cook for 1 minute, or until evenly coated and thickened.

7 To serve, divide steamed rice between bowls and top with the stir-fry. Top each bowl with an egg yolk (if using) and sprinkle with sesame seeds and a few extra scallions.

SUMAC-BRAISED CHICKEN AND ONIONS WITH TAHINI

2ib (900g) bone-in, skin-on chicken thighs and drumsticks

4 garlic cloves, smashed

¾ cup (100g) pine nuts

½ tbsp ground sumac

Fine sea salt and freshly ground black pepper

FOR THE MARINADE

2 tbsps olive oil

1 lemon, thinly sliced

1 tbsp ground sumac

1 tsp ground cardamom

1½ tsps fine sea salt

1 tsp freshly ground black pepper

FOR THE ONIONS

4 large onions, finely diced

1½ tsps fine sea salt

2 cups (500ml) olive oil

1 tbsp ground sumac

1 tsp ground cardamom

1 tsp freshly ground black pepper

TO SERVE

4 large, round flatbreads (such as taboon, pita, or naan)

3 tbsps good-quality tahini

Small bunch of fresh parsley, to garnish

SERVES 4

This dish takes its inspiration from musakhan, a popular Palestinian dish. Commonly served on taboon flatbread, musakhan consists of softened, fragrant onions and a hearty helping of chicken, plus fistfuls of lemony, vibrant sumac. Typically, the chicken is served as whole thighs or drumsticks, but I like to take it a step further and shred the chicken before cooking it down until it's rich and stew-like. Top the whole thing with toasted pine nuts, fresh parsley, and a drizzle of tahini (which isn't a traditional accompaniment, but adds a wonderful nuttiness).

PAIR WITH An American brown ale. The maltiness of the style works well with this dish's deep roasty flavors. But this is also a dish of considerable richness, thanks to the braised chicken and glug of tahini—a generous amount of hop-led bitterness is just the thing to temper it.

THREE BEERS TO TRY Cloudwater Brown Ale (UK); Dogfish Head Indian Brown Ale (US); Mikkeller Jackie Brown Brown Ale (Denmark)

1 Marinate the chicken at least 4–5 hours before cooking, and preferably the night before. Add the chicken and all the marinade ingredients to a large, nonreactive bowl. Mix everything together with your hands until the chicken is evenly coated. Cover and chill in the refrigerator. .

2 Approximately 1 hour before cooking, remove the chicken from the refrigerator to let come to room temperature.

3 Meanwhile, for the onions, add the onions to a large skillet (frying pan) with the sea salt and olive oil (the onions should almost be submerged in the oil). Place over medium-high heat until the oil starts to bubble, then reduce the heat to medium-low and cook for 20–30 minutes, or until the onions are soft but still hold their shape and are just starting to turn golden.

4 Place a sieve over a bowl and drain the onions for 20–30 minutes, stirring gently with a spatula so that as much of the oil is released as possible. (You'll be using this onion-infused oil throughout the recipe, so don't discard it; there will be excess, but it's delicious, and worth chilling and saving for other uses.) Transfer the onions to another bowl and add the sumac, cardamom, and black pepper. Stir gently to combine, and set aside.

(Method continues overleaf)

5 Add 3 tablespoons of the reserved onion-infused oil to a Dutch oven, or a large saucepan with a lid, and place over high heat. Once the oil is very hot, add several of the chicken pieces—you will probably need to do this in two or three batches, so the cooking pot isn't crowded—and cook without disturbing for about 3 minutes, or until the chicken is well browned. Flip and cook on the other side for 2–3 minutes, or until browned. Transfer the chicken to a plate and let rest. Repeat for the remaining batches of chicken.

6 Return the chicken, and any accumulated juices and lemon slices from the marinade, to the cleaned cooking pot and add the garlic. Cover with just-boiled water until the chicken is just submerged (about 4 cups/1 liter). Bring to a boil, then reduce the heat to low and cover. Cook for about 20 minutes, or until the chicken is cooked through and just beginning to fall apart. Transfer the chicken pieces to a cutting board and let rest.

7 Meanwhile, cook the chicken broth, uncovered, on high for 15–20 minutes, or until reduced by half.

8 While the broth is reducing, toast the pine nuts in a small skillet (frying pan) over medium-high heat. Toast, tossing frequently, for approximately 4–5 minutes, or until the pine nuts are golden brown and smell nutty. Remove from the heat and set aside.

9 When the chicken is cool enough to handle, shred the meat roughly with your hands. Discard the skin and bones. Once the broth has reduced significantly, return the chicken to the pot and stir through. Cook over high heat, stirring often to prevent sticking, for a further 15–20 minutes, or until the broth looks rich, stewed, and no longer watery. Stir through several large spoonfuls of the reserved cooked onions. Add the sumac and half the toasted pine nuts, and season to taste. Remove from the heat.

10 Preheat the oven to 400°F/200°C/Gas 6. Line two baking trays with foil and place two flatbreads on each. Brush each flatbread with the onion-infused oil. Divide the remaining cooked onions between the flatbreads and spread into a thin layer. Top with the chicken. Bake for 5–7 minutes or until the edges of the flatbread begin to brown.

11 To serve, drizzle the tahini over the flatbreads, top with the remaining toasted pine nuts, and garnish with the parsley.

BLUEBERRY AND BLACKBERRY COBBLER

FOR THE FILLING

3 cups (450g) blueberries

1¼ cups (190g)
blackberries

½ cup (85g) packed dark
brown sugar

2 tsps vanilla extract

2 tsps ground cinnamon

Zest of 2 lemons

1½ tbsps cornstarch
(cornflour)

FOR THE DOUGH

1½ cups (190g) all-
purpose (plain) flour,
plus extra for dusting

1½ tsps baking powder

¾ tsp fine sea salt

2 tbsps granulated sugar,
plus extra for sprinkling

1 tsp dried culinary
lavender (optional)

5 tbsps (70g) unsalted
butter, chilled and cut
into small cubes

½ cup (125ml) whole milk,
plus extra for brushing

TO SERVE

Vanilla ice cream

SERVES 6

Only slightly more complicated than a crumble, a cobbler is a wonderfully flexible dessert. Though cobblers are usually associated with summer, they can be served all year round and filled with almost any fruit you can get hold of. Here, I use a mix of blueberries and blackberries, scented with cinnamon and vanilla, which bakes down into a beautiful, inky purple. What distinguishes a cobbler from other fruit-filled desserts is its biscuit (scone) topping; I add lavender to the dough to evoke late-summer days.

PAIR WITH A sweet stout, preferably one made with vanilla or berries. Sweet stouts—or pastry stouts, as they're also known—taste like dessert in a glass. Select one with enough of its own sweetness to match the cobbler's fruit and brown sugar.

THREE BEERS TO TRY Evil Twin Imperial Biscotti Break Natale Pretty Please With a Cherry on Top (US); Omnipollo x Dugges Anagram (Sweden); Prairie Artisan Ales Paradise (US)

1 Preheat the oven to 400°F/200°C/Gas 6.

2 To make the filling, add the berries to a baking dish (preferably made from Pyrex or ceramic), measuring approximately 6 x 8 inches (15 x 20cm) and at least 2 inches (5cm) deep. Add the brown sugar, vanilla extract, cinnamon, lemon zest, and cornstarch (cornflour), and mix with a wooden spoon until thoroughly combined. Set aside, and let macerate.

3 Meanwhile, to make the dough, add the flour, baking powder, sea salt, sugar, and lavender (if using) to a medium bowl, and whisk to combine. Add the cubed butter to the flour mixture. Using the tips of your fingers or a pastry cutter, work the butter through the flour until the mixture resembles coarse meal.

4 Pour in the milk and stir with a wooden spoon until a dough forms and there are no floury bits left in the bowl. The dough should be soft, but not too sticky to handle; if it feels very soft, add a small amount of extra flour and mix to incorporate.

5 Flour the work surface. Scoop out the dough and pat into an even rectangle about ½ inch (1cm) thick. Using a biscuit cutter or your half-cup measure, cut out six biscuits (scones)—you may need to re-roll the dough once or twice—and arrange them evenly over the berries. There should ideally be small gaps between the biscuits. Brush the top of each biscuit with a little milk and sprinkle over a pinch of sugar.

6 Bake for approximately 25–35 minutes, pausing to rotate the dish halfway through if your oven has hotspots. The cobbler is finished when the topping is risen and deep golden and the berry mixture is bubbling up through the gaps. Remove from the oven and let cool for about 45 minutes, or until the filling is just set.

7 To serve, divide the cobbler between bowls and top with the vanilla ice cream.

BUTTERSCOTCH CHOCOLATE CHIP COOKIES

2 sticks (225g) unsalted butter, at room temperature

1⅔ cups (210g) all-purpose (plain) flour

¾ cup (65g) rye flour (or use whole-wheat/wholemeal flour)

1 tsp baking soda (bicarbonate of soda)

1 tsp fine sea salt

½ cup (100g) granulated sugar

1 cup (200g) packed light brown sugar

2 tsps vanilla extract

2 eggs

7oz (200g) good-quality semi-sweet (dark) chocolate (minimum 70% cocoa solids), roughly chopped

2oz (55g) butterscotch chips/pieces (optional)

Flaky sea salt (such as Maldon)

MAKES APPROXIMATELY 12 EXTRA-LARGE COOKIES

Simple, nostalgia-suffused chocolate chip cookies are kind of fraught, it turns out. Or at least that's the case if you spend time browsing through recipes online, which seem almost universally competitive in tone, each promising some ultimate Ur-cookie. Me, I'm a gleaner, and this recipe combines a number of my favorite techniques sourced from far and wide. These cookies owe a debt to Jacques Torres; as in his recipe, the dough is aged overnight before baking, the cookies are enormous, and are finished with a crunch of sea salt. They're also made with brown butter (Joy the Baker) and chopped-up chocolate instead of chips (Serious Eats). The result? If not ultimate, then certainly damn good.

PAIR WITH A sweet, dark stout. It's hardly a surprise that chocolate stouts and actual chocolate get along splendidly. Look for a stout with a good amount of its own sweetness, so it can stand up to the sugar in this recipe; stouts flavored with vanilla, coffee, or other dessert-like ingredients also pair well.

THREE BEERS TO TRY Lervig x Hoppin' Frog Sippin' Into Darkness (Norway); Maine Beer Company Mean Old Tom (US); Mikkeller Beer Geek Vanilla Shake (Denmark)

1 First, brown the butter. Slice one stick (115g) of butter and add to a small skillet (frying pan) over medium-high heat. Once melted, cook for about 3–5 minutes, stirring frequently and watching closely until the butter turns a dark golden brown and smells nutty and toasty (it may foam up as it cooks). Once browned, transfer immediately to a heatproof bowl, cover, and put in the refrigerator. Wait until the butter is tepid before using (about 30 minutes).

2 Add both flours, the baking soda (bicarbonate of soda), and sea salt to a medium bowl, and whisk to combine. Set aside.

3 Add the remaining stick of butter and the superfine (caster) sugar to a large bowl and cream together with a hand mixer for 3–4 minutes, or until fluffy and light yellow. Add the cooled brown butter and beat to combine. Add the light brown sugar and beat for a further 1–2 minutes, or until fluffy.

4 Add the vanilla extract and one of the eggs to the wet ingredients, and beat until combined, pausing to scrape down the sides of the bowl if necessary. Add the second egg and beat until whipped and glossy (about 45 seconds).

5 Add the dry ingredients to the wet in one addition and beat on low until just combined, pausing to scrape down the bowl to ensure all the flour is incorporated.

6 Add the chopped chocolate and butterscotch chips/pieces (if using) to the cookie dough, and stir through with a spatula until evenly incorporated. Cover with plastic wrap (clingfilm) and chill in the refrigerator for at least 18 hours (and up to 24 hours).

(Method continues overleaf)

7 The next day, preheat the oven to 325°F/160°C/Gas 3. Line a baking sheet with parchment (baking) paper. Remove the dough from the refrigerator and scoop into roughly 3½-oz (100g) balls, molding loosely into spheres with your hands if the shapes are uneven. (You may need to let the dough warm up slightly before it is scoopable.) Place the cookies, 3 inches (7.5cm) apart, on the lined baking sheet—depending on the size of the sheet, bake the cookies in batches of 4 or 6 cookies at a time, as they spread a good deal. Sprinkle each cookie lightly with flaky sea salt.

8 Bake for approximately 18–20 minutes, rotating the sheet halfway through if your oven has hotspots. The cookies should be golden on the outside and soft on the inside, but not too gooey or raw (they will firm up as they cool, so err toward under-baking). Remove the cookies from the oven and let cool for several minutes before transferring to a cooling rack. Repeat for the remaining batches. Once cooled, the cookies can be stored in an airtight container for up to 5 days.

ACKNOWLEDGMENTS

CLAIRE BULLEN

For starters, thanks to Jen Ferguson for being the best co-author a girl could ever hope for, and for inviting me along on this mad journey. Thanks to Glenn Williams for all of his help and hand-modeling skills. You guys are a dream team. Grateful to Clare Hulton for having our backs, and to Pete Jorgensen and the Dog 'n' Bone team for being so supportive.

So many friends and family members pitched in to make this book possible, and I couldn't be more grateful to them. Thanks to my parents, Martha and Martin Bullen, for help on everything from proposal-writing advice to burger flipping: couldn't have done any of it without you. Thanks to my Uncle Paul Mahon for his legal savvy and encouragement all the way through. Thanks to my brother, Stuart Bullen, for excellent beer input and recipe-testing know-how. Sharona Selby, editor extraordinaire and recipe-testing maven, has earned my eternal gratitude. Josh Smith gets a big shout-out for all of his brilliant design work and recipe-testing skills, and we couldn't have done any of it without Matt Curtis, who took beautiful photos, advised on beer choices, and, in introducing me and the HB&B crew, made everything happen. Thanks as well to Anna Malkan for her tablescaping talents and recipe-testing work, and to Sofia Ed Larsen and Dror Asaf for being photoshoot guest-stars. Thanks to Ned Palmer for his infinite cheese wisdom, and to my roommates—Sam Mansell and Solène Louat—for putting up with all of my kitchen tomfoolery. A special shout-out to Arianna Halshaw (@ahceramics) who kindly let us borrow her beautiful platters.

Massive kudos to my fleet of other brilliant recipe testers. Thanks to Leah Riley Brown, Zef Cherry-Kynaston, Eli Lee, Katie Manning-Cork, Katie Marcus, Alan McQuade, Sri Mohan, Susan Narewski, Marek Narkiewicz, Ann O'Donoghue, Jimmy Ogden, Phill Palgrave-Elliott, Steph Palgrave-Elliott, Rekha Shankar, Devon Snyder, Jess Stone, Isabella Styles, Nicole Valentine, and Kate Waters. You're all gems.

JEN FERGUSON

The biggest thanks go to Claire Bullen, who did most of the heavy lifting on this book while I just got to waffle on about beer. Big cheers also to all those beer lovers around the world who we called on for international beer tips and industry insights, with particular thanks to Jono Galuszka, Phil Clement, Stuart Bullen, Stu McKinlay, and HB&B team member Joris Gort. Thanks to all the brewers, everywhere, for making great beer, but specifically to all of the brewers mentioned in this book who graciously gave up their time to talk with me. Huge thanks to our design guru Samuel Muir for his wonderful style guidance as ever. Matthew Curtis is a rock star both behind the camera and the computer—nice one, fella. And, of course, eternal thanks to the fabulous Glenn Williams, who went along with this crazy idea to open a beer, hot sauce, and records shop in South London all those years ago.

INDEX